Deconstructing Discovery

Tactics, Talk Tracks and Transcripts -
Your Actionable Step-By-Step Guide to Running
Discovery Calls Like a Pro

MARK ACKERS AND RICHARD SMITH

Praise for Deconstructing Discovery

Anthony Parker, CRO, Forecast

"With Deconstructing Discovery, Mark and Rich deliver a real-world blueprint that, if applied, will accelerate a rep's performance, experience, and earnings by years. This is essential reading for every aspiring or established AE."

Elaine Tyler, CEO, Venatrix

"This book turns good sellers into exceptional ones with practical, deal-closing insights. I'm getting everyone on my go-to-market team a copy."

Chris Dawson, Director and Sales Trainer, 6th Door

"Essential reading for anyone conducting discovery and wanting to take their sales game to the next level. If you buy one sales book this year, make sure it's this."

Ollie Sharpe, CRO, Trumpet

"A sales bible that belongs on every desk - this book nails why discovery matters most. It's packed with practical insights, proven talk tracks, and after reading it once I realised I need to read it again - it's that kind of book!"

Katie Miles, Senior Mid-Market AE, Navan

"This is the ultimate Sales 101 playbook - no fluff, just golden, enforceable tactics. It's packed with exact phrases and leaves you wanting more."

Steve Myers, Sales Coach, MySalesCoach & Founder, Human Aligned Sales

"This book blends psychology, technology, and decades of sales wisdom into a must-have manual. It's already earned a place on my 'move the needle' book shelf."

Chris Russell, Head of Sales Development, VinciWorks

"Most books tell you what to say-this one shows you how to apply it. The full discovery transcripts are a total game-changer."

Sophie Allen, Founder, Trampoline

"This book helped me rethink and upgrade my discovery process overnight. The advice is practical, no-fluff, and instantly effective.""

Bruno Broughton, Head of Business Development, Synthesia

"The examples are accurate, the talk tracks are universal, and the advice is built to last. This book will be by my side for the next decade."

James Ski, Founder, Sales Confidence

"This book gives you the full toolkit of questions needed to run powerful discovery calls. Huge congrats to Mark and Richard for capturing so much real-world value."

Ashley Ormond, Sales Development Leader

"Don't just talk-discover. This no-fluff guide will make your sales conversations convert."

Holly Allen, Founding AE UK&I, FullEnrich

"Finally, a step-by-step guide that makes discovery clear, simple, and effective. I'm calling it my new discovery bible."

Sian Taylor, Sales Manager, Klaviyo

"When pipeline is tight, you need discovery to hit harder-this book delivers exactly that. It's your one-stop shop for the entire sales cycle."

Jack Frimston, Co-Director, We Have a Meeting

"This is the most in-depth, practical guide to discovery I've seen. Grounded in real-life examples and built for reps who want results."

Will Aitken, Founder, Sales As F*ck

"Discovery usually gets explained like theory-these guys make it real. You get the what, the why, and exactly how to do it."

Dave Kurlan, CEO, Kurlan & Associates

"Clear examples, talk tracks, and frameworks every seller can apply immediately. Everyone in sales, regardless of experience level and role, will benefit from reading this book."

Gerry Hill, GM, ConnectAndSell

"This book helps sellers at every level reconnect with the fundamentals. The inclusion of GPT prompts is a fresh, relevant, and playful twist."

Carly Pledge, Enterprise Sales Director, Datamaran

"This is discovery done right - packed with real tactics that work. A must-read for any AE or Sales Leader"

Dougie Loan, CRO, Sourcewhale

"This book goes way beyond discovery-it's a universal sales playbook for AEs at every level. Read it, apply it, and watch your performance skyrocket."

Cory Bray, Co-Founder, CoachCRM

"This book bridges the gap between theory and the real world. Every concept is grounded in sound principles and real-life sales scenarios."

Tara Jackson, AE, Swap

"All the discovery advice you need is here-and it's incredibly easy to put into action. This book will elevate every conversation you have."

Zac Thompson, Co-Founder, We Have a Meeting

"This book gives you fresh strategies and a new mindset - the kind that helps you shift gears for your entire career."

For anyone who bought Problem Prospecting?! as an SDR and has transitioned to become an AE.

Who gets on a discovery call expecting a conversation - only to get vague answers and objections

Who watches deals stall for months while your boss asks, "What's the next step?"

Who's had a CFO wreck their forecast with a single email

Who's been told, "This isn't a priority right now" more times than they can count

Who thought they'd nailed a discovery call - only to be completely ghosted, and left wondering what went wrong

Who thought closing would be easy - until they realised getting a prospect to commit is a whole new ball game

This one's for you...

Foreword

"I lost a great project to a cheaper competitor," a seller from a video production company told me.

He was really pissed.

"The thing that really annoys me is they told me their budget. I knew we could do the best job for whatever their budget was, and they told me exactly what their budget was.

I know we could do a much better job. I know they'll be disappointed with the outcome."

I could tell he thought the buyer had screwed up.

"Can I be honest with you?" I asked.

He nodded, I'm sure still anticipating that we'd agree buyers are stupid or something.

"This is your fault," I told him.

I saw the shock in his face. How could it be his fault? He had done exactly what the prospect wanted. He was convinced they had the best proposal. He was sure they had the best team to deliver the best outcome. How the hell was this 'my' fault, his face said, with a look of both bewilderment and anger.

"Tell me, is this the first time this has happened?" I asked.

He confirmed it was not. In fact, it has happened many times.

"And why has this happened to you?"

"Prospects lie. Sometimes their boss just wants to save money. And they don't realise that we will give them the best outcome they are looking for."

"You're losing these deals with missteps in your discovery," I told him.

Prospects lie.

Other people influence deals.

You don't understand the pain and true desired outcome, or the reasons it matters.

You've not demonstrated the value and differentiation to make an informed decision.

There was probably much more. But this deal was clearly lost in discovery.

In fact, most deals are. And whether resulting in a competitor being chosen, failure to get budget, other stakeholders derailing or just no decision before they started ghosting you, the deals were all likely lost long ago at the discovery stage.

It may have been the things you did. But most likely it was the things you didn't.

Mark and Rich, the authors of this book learned this, not just through their own personal experiences - as significant as they will have been. We all shared the most privileged front row seat.

Tens of thousands of discovery calls across sectors, deal sizes, sales processes and methodologies. The best sales teams and their Presidents Club performers, to the teams still writing the playbooks and the reps who never make it through PIPs.

We saw the data. We heard the calls. As co-founders and leaders at a Revenue Intelligence platform, we had exclusive seats that exposed us to the discovery calls that others would never be exposed to across multiple lifetimes.

And that's why *'Deconstructing Discovery'* will be truly game changing to your sales outcomes or your teams.

We've got the band back together and founded MySalesCoach, driven by a goal to help sellers and teams achieve success and reach their potential. It's not just a startup. It is a mission.

Mark and Richard have lived and breathed this world for the last 30 collective years.

While *'Problem Prospecting?!'* achieved best-selling success and became a bible for BDRs and quota carriers alike, the value of *'Deconstructing Discovery'* will be even more profound I am sure. Because while prospecting is clearly critical to the scale of sales success, deals are won and lost in discovery.

Devour this book. Your future pipeline, career and wealth will thank you.

Kevin Beales

Co-founder and CEO (with Mark at MySalesCoach and previously Rich at Refract)

Thanks...

With great appreciation to...

Kevin Beales for his foreword and encouragement in helping us put this book together.

The whole MySalesCoach team for their support in helping us launch the book.

Tom Boston for designing the front cover.

And to our collective families for giving us the time to write it.

Table of Contents

Introduction

Five years ago, we wrote *'Problem Prospecting?!'* as a side project during lockdown. At the time, we had no idea how much impact it would have. To our surprise, the book resonated with sales professionals worldwide, selling over 7,000 copies (at the time of writing) and continuing to sell daily in nearly every continent. The response was a testament to the need for real, actionable sales advice that cuts through the fluff and delivers practical guidance.

The feedback we received was clear - people appreciated the fact that the book didn't just tell them what to do, but also showed them how to do it. Many sales books offer vague, strategic advice without providing the practical, actionable steps that sellers need to succeed. We set out to change that, and the response confirmed we were onto something. The ongoing demand for *Problem Prospecting?!* has shown us just how vital it is for sales professionals to have a resource that is both immediately applicable and deeply relevant to their day-to-day challenges.

Since then, the sales landscape has changed dramatically. Virtual sales interactions have become the norm, whereas going into 2020 (pre-Covid), face-to-face selling was still dominant. More importantly, buyer expectations have shifted, and the balance of power in the sales (or buying) process has tilted even further in favour of the buyer. Traditional sales methodologies and outdated processes are no longer enough - sellers need to evolve to meet modern buyer demands. Salespeople are expected to provide more value than ever before; they need to be consultative, insightful, and capable of guiding a buyer toward a decision in a way that feels natural, rather than forced.

Despite these changes, one fundamental truth remains; sales are won and lost in the conversations sellers have with buyers. In an increasingly crowded market, where products and services often seem indistinguishable, the ability to lead high-quality sales conversations is what sets the best apart from the rest. Buyers today have more access to information than ever before; they also have more choices, and higher expectations. Simply having a great product or service isn't enough anymore - what makes the real difference is the way you engage with a prospect and uncover their needs.

We have had the benefit of speaking with literally thousands of Sales Leaders over the past decade. They say things like:

- "We lose too many deals to no decision."
- "Our competition are taking our market share."
- "My salespeople are too quick to discount."
- "Our conversion rates need to improve."
- "Prospects just ghost us too often."
- "Our salespeople are losing deals they should be winning."

The truth is, all of these things are heavily impacted by a salesperson's inability to have great conversations with their buyers.

Our journey at Refract, a conversation intelligence SaaS company, reinforced this belief. Going up against better-funded, larger competitors, we had to find a way to differentiate ourselves beyond just our product. We became obsessed with our sales interactions - analysing them, practicing them, and continually improving. Our ability to create exceptional buying experiences helped us punch above our weight and ultimately led to a successful exit from the business. We saw first-hand that a great conversation could be the difference between winning and losing a deal, and that companies that mastered this skill had a significant competitive advantage.

We spent hours listening to our own discovery calls, giving each other feedback, deconstructing them in team sessions, and even reviewing them during everyday moments like commuting or walking the dog. Mastering sales conversations wasn't just an initiative - it was an obsession that made all the difference. By dedicating time to understanding what made a great conversation and how to continuously improve, we were able to drive results that enabled us to stay competitive.

After Refract, our years in enterprise software sales only reinforced what we had long suspected: most companies still weren't dedicating enough time to improve sales conversations, despite their undeniable impact. Sales coaching was rarely prioritised, leaving sellers without the guidance they needed to elevate their effectiveness. That's why we started MySalesCoach - to give sellers the coaching they crave and deserve. Sales teams need ongoing, personalised coaching to bridge the gap between knowing what to do and actually executing it effectively.

We noticed a familiar problem though. Just as we saw before we wrote *'Problem Prospecting?!'* salespeople were constantly being told to "do deeper discovery," "ask better questions," "multi-thread more" and "bring more value to prospects." But too often, they were left wondering how to actually do these things. Similarly, most sales books deliver high level strategic information, but lack the true step-by-step guidance that people need. Sellers don't need more high-level theories. They need practical, replicable frameworks they can apply immediately in their conversations with buyers. That's the gap we are aiming to fill with this book.

'Deconstructing Discovery' is the product of years of studying, practicing, and refining sales conversations. We have distilled our learnings (and mistakes!) into an actionable playbook designed to help modern B2B sellers master the most critical part of the sales process - discovery conversations. We break down what makes a great discovery call, how to uncover genuine buyer pain points, how to navigate complex decision making, and how to structure your conversations for maximum impact.

This book will provide you with real-world strategies, practical tactics, simplified analysis and historical transcripts from our own sales calls. It's designed to move beyond abstract sales advice and give you the tools to truly excel in discovery conversations. By the end, you won't just understand why great discovery matters - you'll know exactly how to execute it effectively in your own sales process.

This may sound a little strange, but for many of you, reading this book cover-to-cover may not be the smartest option. Much like our first book, we want you to see this as a handy guide to keep on your desk before you jump on a call with a prospect. Flick to the chapter that you feel will be most beneficial for you based on the situation you are in. Choose the pages that will give you the right guidance at the right time. See this as a playbook versus a story.

We're so excited to share this journey with you. Without further ado, let's get started.

Chapter One

What a Discovery Call Is (and What It's Not)

I'm not entirely sure where and when the term *"discovery call"* originated. My hunch is that it's a term which has evolved from the bubble that is SaaS sales. If you don't call them discovery calls, perhaps instead you call them:

- Information Gathering Calls.
- Introductory Calls.
- First meetings.
- Consultations.
- Initial Diagnostics.

Whatever you frame them as, they all essentially relate to the same thing.

Perhaps rather than asking what a discovery call is, a better question to ask is, *"What is the objective of this initial conversation?"* From there, it really helps us understand the key purpose of these critical interactions with our prospects.

Refer to a dictionary, and this is what you will uncover:

Discovery - the process of finding information

While that is true of a sales discovery call, it definitely sells things short.

Because while doing great discovery with a prospect definitely includes *"finding information"* about their world, their situation, and their problems, simply finding out information suggests a one-way street of you asking lots of questions, and your prospect providing lots of answers.

Indeed this is where my whole thoughts and opinions on discovery have evolved over the years, in light of how companies buy and the buying preferences of our prospects.

This is what discovery should *not* look like:

- A one-way street of you (the seller) asking your prospect lots of questions and your prospect giving lots of answers.

- The opposite situation of your prospect asking you lots of questions, and you (the seller) giving lots of answers.

- A one-off interaction (discovery should be an ongoing process).

- A conversation where your prospect leaves the meeting feeling you got everything you wanted but they learned very little.

- A thinly veiled sales pitch where you end up telling your prospect all of the great things about you and your company.

In fact, I recently asked a buyer about what goes through their head when they are buying something, and how important the effectiveness of the salesperson is for them in making a decision.

This was their answer:

"I need to get the feeling that the person in front of me understands my world. If that person does not understand my world, I instantly lose any sort of trust that this person is going to help me find the right solution, even if the product might be great."

To understand your prospect's world, you *have* to be effective at discovery.

The point is, discovery should ultimately feel like a mutually beneficial conversation where, above anything else, your prospect leaves the conversation feeling that you understood their world.

Too often, discovery falls down on one or many of the above points, so the very basics of building trust and rapport between seller and buyer disintegrate before you even get started. We are going to get into the highly tactical elements of discovery in this book, but it's important to have an appreciation of the basics before you get started.

So what is the purpose of discovery?

Well after 15+ years of selling, I've ended up reflecting and boiling it down to having clear answers to the following questions:

- Does the prospect have a problem I can solve?
- How big is the problem?
- Why does the prospect care about investing time, effort, and money solving the problem now (or at the very least in the short term)?

- Why am I better positioned to solve the problem than somebody else?

When you lay it out like that, it looks and feels quite straightforward, doesn't it?

While the critical concept of discovery, which so few people in sales are genuinely strong at, makes or breaks sales success, it looks like a piece of cake[1].

Well... perhaps not. (And that's why we wrote this book!)

But actually, when I think back to all the deals I've closed over the years, I was very clear on the answers to the above questions. And the deals which dragged on and on to *"no decision"*, I had very unclear answers to some or all of the above questions.

Let's break down each of these in more detail:

1. Does the prospect have a problem I can solve?

Does the prospect tell you that they are suffering a problem that you help solve or are you trying to create problems that don't exist?

2. How big is the problem?

Is the problem something that truly bothers the prospect enough for them to want to spend time, money, and effort solving it?

---

1. Objective Management Group's data states that only 6% of all salespeople are classified as "strong" at consultative selling.

3. **Why does the prospect care about solving the problem now (or at the very least in the short term)?**

Is the prospect motivated to actually want to take action to solve the problem quickly?

4. **Why am I better positioned to solve the problem than somebody else?**

What makes you specifically different and makes you a more compelling option to solve the problem for the prospect, as opposed to your competition (or even the option of them just trying to fix it themselves)?

Later on in this book, we will dive into these four questions in greater detail.

For now though, when it's laid out like that - doing great discovery looks to be pretty straightforward doesn't it?

And I guess when you break it down into a simple format, it is.

But the truth is, so many people struggle with this critical piece of the sales/buying cycle.

That's because the intricacies of HOW you get the answers to the above questions is where things can get more complex. It always comes down to the execution.

And much like our reasons for writing Problem *Prospecting?!* back in 2020, we have found that many sellers have never actually been taught HOW to execute They are just simply told to "have great discovery conversations with prospects" or to "bring the value", but aren't actually shown HOW to do it.

I will finish this chapter by making sure the following is understood loud and clear.

We are living in a fast-changing world of B2B sales, where the expectations from buyers have never been higher.

In fact, data shows that an increasing majority of buyers would prefer to not even have to deal with a salesperson AT ALL when it comes to buying something.

We can all probably relate this to our personal lives, where buying something in two clicks on an app on our phone is much more desirable than having to walk into a store and be met with an assistant who asks us, "What are you looking for today?"

As such, the challenge for salespeople when it comes to discovery is ensuring that, at the very least, buyers are coming away from a conversation feeling like it was a worthy use of their time. Even when you establish you aren't a great fit for your prospect, consider how you can make the discovery call feel like it wasn't a total waste of 30/45/60 minutes. You never know when you may become a better fit for the prospect. Timing is everything in sales. So ensure you at least remain somewhat memorable. We'll dive into how you are able to do this in this book.

OK, now that's out of the way, it's time to get started with preparation...

Chapter Two

Preparing For your Discovery Call

The Importance of Preparation

One of the biggest challenges created by the virtual selling culture is that salespeople are constantly jumping on discovery calls with little to no preparation. We've all been there - scrambling at the last minute, glancing at a LinkedIn profile or re-reading a CRM note just moments before the call starts. The result? Lazy selling, disengaged conversations, and a lack of prospect-centricity.

Whenever I have gone on to a call underprepared, and watched the call back afterwards, it really showed.

But preparation is what separates great salespeople from the rest. When you take the time to truly understand your prospect, their business, and their challenges, you set yourself up to have a meaningful, impactful conversation. You show up as a professional who has done their homework, not just another salesperson looking to push a product. Not only that, but there is so much freely accessible information about our prospects and their organisations today, that not leveraging this to your advantage is a wasted opportunity.

That's why I've developed the **PPREPCOO** framework - a simple, actionable method that will help you structure your preparation so that every discovery call is productive and valuable for both you and your prospect. This framework is designed to take just **15-20 minutes**, yet the impact it has on your calls can be transformative. Great preparation can help influence the way you start your conversations, the questions you ask, and ultimately your mindset with respect to the direction you want discovery calls to take.

The PPREPCOO Framework

PPREPCOO stands for:

- **P** - Personal Profile: Understanding the prospect's background and professional identity.
- **P** - Purpose: What is the agreed purpose of the discovery call with each participant?
- **R** - Recent Activity: Analysing what they've been up to, what they have been engaging with and what they have been discussing publicly.
- **E** - Experience: Examining their career trajectory and role responsibilities.
- **P** - Past Interactions: Reviewing any previous touchpoints with your company.
- **C** - Company News: Researching the latest updates and priorities at their company.
- **O** - Other Similar Customers: Leveraging social proof to build credibility.
- **O** - Outcomes: What decisions will be made at the end of the call?

Each of these elements plays a crucial role in ensuring that you're well-prepared and ready to lead an insightful discovery conversation. By following the PPREPCOO* framework, you ensure that your call is focused on the prospect's needs rather than a generic sales pitch.

Deep Dive into PPREPCOO

1. Personal Profile (P)

The first place to start is your prospect's LinkedIn profile. A quick look at their profile can reveal a wealth of information that can be leveraged to build rapport and craft relevant questions. When reviewing their profile, focus on:

- Their headline and summary: What do they emphasise about themselves? Are they focused on growth, innovation, efficiency, or leadership?
- Achievements and key milestones: Do they highlight accomplishments or results that they're proud of?
- Passions and focus areas: Do they mention any key initiatives they're leading?
- Personal insights - Tools like Crystal Knows can give you an idea of their personality type, which can help you adjust your communication style accordingly. Are they direct and to-the-point, or do they prefer a more relationship-driven approach? If you try to go into lots of detail with a "High D" then you are going to be met with strong resistance. Equally, if you are too direct

too quickly with someone who is softer and more compliant, then you are going to make them feel uncomfortable. Elite selling involves being able to adapt your approach to get on the same level as the prospect you are speaking with

By understanding these elements, you can tailor your approach and ensure you engage them in a manner that aligns with their professional identity.

Example Questions:

- *"I noticed in your profile that you have a passion for coaching sales reps. What are some of the hardest things you find about coaching?"*
- *"I saw that you were recently promoted - congratulations! What are your top focuses in this new role?"*

ChatGPT Prompt: *"Summarise the key responsibilities and strategic priorities of someone in a [prospect's job title] role at a company like [company name]."*

2. Purpose (P)

One of the most overlooked (yet critical) parts of preparation is getting absolute clarity on **why this call is happening** - and why it matters to the person on the other end. Purpose isn't just about *your* reason for being there. It's about *their* reason too.

Before the call, ask yourself:

- What is the agreed purpose of this conversation?
- What are they expecting to get out of it?
- What would success look like from their perspective?

This clarity allows you to align your flow, questions, and tone with their expectations - and avoid veering off track. It also helps you stay outcome-focused without being overly rigid.

Tip: When you're booking the meeting or confirming it, explicitly ask:

"So we're aligned, what would make this call valuable for you?"

Having that answer in your notes gives you an anchor to return to throughout the conversation.

Example Questions:

- *"Just to check, what do you want to make sure we have covered by the end of the call today ?"*
- *"I want to make sure we use our time wisely - what prompted you to take the meeting now?"*

3. Recent Activity (R)

One of the most overlooked areas of preparation is Recent Activity on LinkedIn. This tells you what's top of mind for your prospect right now. Even if they don't post frequently, check for:

- Posts they've written or shared: Are they discussing industry trends or challenges?
- Comments they've left on others' posts: What opinions or insights are they engaging with?
- Company announcements they've reacted to: Are they involved in a major initiative at their company?

Looking at recent activity can give you strong hints about their current challenges, priorities, and interests, allowing you to structure your questions accordingly.

One recent example of this happened when I noticed that a VP of Sales had posted about an internal sales workshop they had been running on MEDDPICC. Immediately, I was thinking about why they had been doing that. What were they trying to accomplish by running a workshop? What had been the trigger that had made them invest a ton of time and resources to carry out the workshop in the first place? All perfect questions to ask at the start of my discovery call

Example Questions:

- *"I saw you commented on [industry trend]. What's your take on how that will impact your team?"*
- *"You recently shared a post about [company initiative]. How does that fit into things you're currently looking to tackle?"*

ChatGPT Prompt: *"Analyse the last three LinkedIn posts from [prospect name] and suggest conversation starters based on their content."*

4. Experience (E)

The Experience section on LinkedIn can provide some of the most valuable insights for your discovery call. Take note of:

- Their current role: Do they have a detailed job description? This can tell you what they prioritise in their role.
- Career trajectory: Have they recently been promoted? Were they brought in to lead a specific transformation or initiative?
- Industry shifts: Have they moved between different industries? This can indicate how they approach problems and whether they have a fresh perspective on their current role.

Interestingly, I recently saw that a prospect of mine - a VP of Account Management - had previously been a teacher. So I reasonably assumed that they would be passionate about learning, development, and growth. These were all things which tied into the MySalesCoach proposition. It made me feel like there was a good chance I would have a strong advocate before I had even jumped on a call with them.

Example Questions:

- *"I noticed you joined [company] about six months ago - what were some of the key objectives you were brought in to achieve?"*

- *"You've been with the business for over a year now. What have you learnt about your team in that time?"*
- *"Your previous role at [company] focused on [responsibility]. How does that compare to what you're doing now?"*

5. Past Interactions (P)

One thing that always surprises me is how often salespeople fail to check the CRM before a discovery call. There's simply no excuse for this. The CRM holds a treasure trove of insights - previous conversations, objections, reasons why the prospect didn't move forward earlier, or even what content they've engaged with. Skipping this step means missing out on crucial context that could help build rapport and tailor the conversation. Even worse, it can make you look unprepared and disengaged, forcing the prospect to repeat information they've already communicated. Taking just a few minutes to review past interactions can completely change the trajectory of your call.

Before the call, check your CRM for any past interactions between your company and the prospect. Key things to look for:

- Previous conversations: Have they spoken with a sales rep before? If so, what was discussed? Will they remember the conversation? What stopped them from moving forward last time? Why is now potentially better timing?
- Engagement with your marketing: Another key aspect that often goes overlooked is the types of

marketing content the prospect has engaged with. If they've downloaded a white paper, attended a webinar, or engaged with specific case studies, it's a strong signal about their pain points and interests. This information can help you craft more targeted questions and guide the conversation toward areas where they're already showing curiosity. Additionally, prospects who have interacted with marketing materials have a higher level of familiarity with your brand and a stronger sense of brand equity. This means they may already have preconceived notions, expectations, or questions about your solution. A well-prepared salesperson can leverage this familiarity by acknowledging their previous engagement and seamlessly tying it into the discovery conversation, creating a more meaningful and productive discussion.

- Objections raised previously: Understanding past concerns helps you proactively address them.

Example Questions

- *"I noticed you attended our webinar on [topic]. What were your key takeaways?"*
- *"You spoke with my colleague last year about [product]. What's changed since then that made you interested in revisiting this conversation?"*

6. Company News (C)

Another critical, but often overlooked aspect of preparation is researching company news. Salespeople frequently neglect this, yet it can provide a wealth of insight into a company's strategic priorities, challenges, and direction. Leadership changes, funding announcements, major product launches, or acquisitions can all significantly impact a company's focus and potential pain points.

Referencing company news during a discovery call makes you sound well-informed, and it ensures that your questions are relevant and timely. For example, if a company has recently expanded into a new market, you could ask how that expansion is affecting their team's priorities. If they've just received a new round of funding, you can explore whether they are investing in new tools or initiatives to support growth. If their CEO has just been quoted in an interview saying that they are looking to generate more revenue from new products, then you can start to think about how your value proposition connects to that C-Level strategic initiative.

Using tools like ChatGPT, Google News, or AI-driven research tools can help you quickly summarise company reports, investor updates, and executive interviews. These insights allow you to position your product or service in a way that directly aligns with the company's focus right now, increasing the likelihood of a successful conversation.

Example Questions:

- *"I saw your CEO recently announced a major initiative around [topic]. How is that impacting your team?"*

- *"Your company recently secured funding - how is that influencing your priorities for this year?"*

ChatGPT Prompt: *"Summarise key strategic priorities from recent earnings reports and press releases for [company name]. Please profile those priorities that will link with [problem that my product solves]."*

7. Other Similar Customers (O)

Another key step in preparation is researching similar companies that have faced challenges like those of your prospect. Many salespeople overlook this, but it can be a game-changer. If a prospect sees that a competitor or a peer in their industry is already using your solution, it can create a strong sense of urgency, and even fear of missing out (FOMO). Companies don't want to be left behind, especially when their competitors are adopting new strategies or technologies to gain an advantage.

Looking at similar companies also helps you refine your approach. Instead of asking broad discovery questions, you can reference real-world examples of how other companies have tackled the same problems. You can say something like, "We recently helped [Company X] solve [specific issue], and I'd love to explore whether that experience is relevant to you." This not only builds credibility but also makes the conversation more engaging and relevant to the prospect's situation.

By referring to examples of similar customers, you can validate the business case for your prospect, demonstrate expertise, and position your offering as a tried-and-true solution within their industry.

Example Questions:

- *"We've been working with [competitor] to help their team solve [challenge]. Have you faced similar challenges?"*
- *"Companies in [prospect's industry] often struggle with [problem]. How does that align with your experience?"*

8. Outcomes (O)

Too many discovery calls end with vague next steps - or worse, no direction at all. That's why one of the final pieces of your preparation should be thinking about **what good looks like at the end of the call.**

Before you join, get clear on:

- What decisions do we want to walk away with?
- What would a successful outcome look like for both sides?
- What's the minimum viable next step, and what's the ideal?

Going in with clear, realistic outcome goals helps you guide the conversation with purpose - without being pushy. It also ensures you're steering toward commitment, not just connection.

If you're expecting a demo to be booked, a multi-threading intro, or a deeper technical call, know that in advance. Be ready to frame that next step as a natural conclusion to the conversation.

Example Questions:

- *"Assuming this is relevant, are you open to scheduling time to dive deeper with [X person]?"*
- *"By the end of this call, is it fair to say we'll know whether it makes sense to keep the conversation going?"*

By following PPREPCOO, you'll enter every discovery call prepared, confident, and ready to have more relevant and purposeful conversations. Taking the extra time to research your prospect's background, activity, and experiences will ensure stronger relationships, deeper conversations, and ultimately, better sales outcomes

Now, go PPREPCOO your next discovery call and set yourself up for success!

*One of the benefits of working at MySalesCoach is the unrivaled access we have to some of the best brains in sales. We would like to provide a nod of acknowledgement here to one of our coaches Steve Myers who helped us fine tune this framework!

Chapter Three

Set-up

For many AE's, particularly those stepping into the role for the first time, the focus is on learning how to run a great discovery call, ask better questions, and manage objections. But what is often overlooked is how you set yourself up for success before you even say a word.

Sales is about control. If your set-up is chaotic, and if you are fumbling through tabs, scrambling for notes, or missing key details, you are already losing control.

This chapter is all about the fundamentals of set-up. Get these right, and you will not only sound more confident, but you will actually be more confident. Let's get into it.

1. Your Digital Set-up: Get Your Screen Right

Most discovery calls are run remotely. That means your screen set-up matters. If you are constantly switching tabs, minimising and maximising windows, or losing track of what is where, you are going to look unprepared.

Here is how to fix that:

- **Use a Dual-Screen Set-up**. If possible, have one screen dedicated to your notes and the call itself - this allows you to type while maintaining eye contact. The other screen is for key tabs.

- **Key Tabs**. Before the call starts, make sure you have:

    - ☐ The prospect's LinkedIn profile for quick references.
    - ☐ Any previous correspondence such as emails or CRM notes.
    - ☐ Useful tools like percentagecalculator.com for quick maths.
    - ☐ Your own calendar in case next steps need to be scheduled on the spot

- **Turn Off Self-View**. Seeing yourself on screen is a distraction. You will instinctively check your appearance rather than focus on the prospect. Hide your own video feed and focus on them.

2. The Right Tools at Your Fingertips

A well-prepared AE does not waste time searching for things mid-call. Here are three simple tools that will make your life easier:

PercentageCalculator.com.

Ever had a prospect share numbers, and you weren't sure what they actually meant? For example, *"Our marketing inbound leads generate £75K in revenue, but we need £100K a month to hit the plan."* With percentagecalculator.com, you can instantly see that's a 33% increase - not 25%, which many mistakenly assume.

Being able to state that confidently positions you as a trusted advisor rather than someone guessing at the maths.

Another key advantage? When you highlight the real percentage, prospects often realise just how big the gap is - making them even more aware of the challenge and more likely to see the need for your help.

PronounceNames.com

Nothing kills credibility faster than mispronouncing someone's name. If in doubt, check before the call. If you are still unsure, ask them at the start of the meeting: "I want to make sure I get this right, is it [Name]?" Nobody minds you checking, they mind you getting it wrong.

ChatGPT

If you are speaking to someone in an unfamiliar industry or they use jargon-heavy language, have ChatGPT ready. If they throw out technical terms, drop them into ChatGPT to get a quick, simplified explanation so you do not get caught on the back foot.

3. A Professional (and Distraction-Free) Background

Your background says a lot about you. A messy, unmade bed, piles of laundry, or a dimly lit space signals unprofessionalism. Yes, it may sound silly but I've seen backgrounds like this far too often. When you have a messy background, your prospects make subconscious judgments based on how you present yourself.

- **If you have a professional home office, use it**. A clean, well-lit space with a simple background works best.

- **If not, use a virtual background or a simple blur effect**. No distractions, no bad impressions.

- **Bad virtual background examples**:
  - ☐ Low-quality, pixelated images that make it obvious you are using a background.
  - ☐ Distracting or irrelevant settings such as a beach or outer space.
  - ☐ Backgrounds with company branding that look unnatural or block your shoulders.
  - ☐ Poorly positioned virtual backgrounds where parts of your body disappear when you move.

- **Lighting matters**. A dark, shadowy face makes you look disengaged. Invest in a ring light or position yourself near a window.

4. Always Record Your Calls (and Use the Data)

Recording your discovery calls is not just for reference; it is also for growth. If you are not recording, you are relying on memory; given the amount of words exchanged on a discovery call your memory is not good enough. Nobody's memory is!

Why Record?

- Re-listen for key details. Prospects drop valuable insights all the time. If you miss them, you miss opportunities.

- Extract exact phrasing. The best sellers use their prospects' own words back at them. You cannot do this if you do not capture what they say.
- Use AI for summaries. Transcripts and AI tools can summarise key takeaways, highlight sentiment, and even suggest follow-up questions.

How to Ask for Permission: Most companies now record calls as standard, but if you need to ask, keep it casual:

"Just to check, do you mind if I record this? I have terrible handwriting and a bad memory, and I want to make sure I am fully focused on you rather than scribbling notes."

Almost everyone will say yes.

5. Get Your Prospect on Camera

Body language tells you a lot. If you are running a call with a black screen on the other side, you are missing key signals.

- Always ask them to turn their camera on, but do it smoothly.
- Instead of saying, "Can you turn your camera on?", try:

"I can hear you, but I cannot see you."

Then pause.

Most people will instinctively turn their camera on. If they do not, respect that, but always give them the nudge.

Final Thought: Control the Controllables

You cannot control how a prospect reacts. You cannot control their budget, priorities, or decision-making process. But you can control how well set up and prepared you are.

Most AEs do some of the above, but few do them all. Get your set-up right, and you immediately give yourself an edge over 90 percent of sellers.

Chapter Four

Getting Started

There's a saying: "it's not how you start that's important, but how you finish." While that might be applicable in some situations, it couldn't be any further from the truth when it comes to discovery calls.

The start of the discovery call is arguably the most important. Get it right and you've given yourself the best chance of having a great conversation with your prospect. Get it wrong and it can be extremely hard to recover.

Here's a step-by-step guide on how to start your discovery calls.

Step 1: Prepare your agenda.

Before every call, I write down my agenda and my first line of questions. I must have written it down 1,000 times, it reads as follows:

- Small talk - [observation/topic here]
- Time check
- Agenda

  - ☐ How we got here.
  - ☐ What's the reason we're talking today?

☐ What do they want to get from the conversation?
☐ Ask some questions.
☐ Two outcomes.
- Sounds fair?

And below that I write:

- Talk about the story so far, how we got here.
- Ask what the reason we're talking today is.
- Clarify what they want to get from the conversation.
- How does this link to their goals (professional and personal)?
- Why can't they do this already or with an alternative?
- What happens if this problem isn't solved?
- Who else cares about solving this problem?
- What are the next steps?

I find writing my agenda fresh each time jogs my muscle memory and gets me ready for the call. It's like my warm up routine. I feel confident once I write it down. Copying and pasting it just wouldn't have the same effect on my brain.

Step 2: Small talk

You'll have noticed I put [observation/topic here] next to small talk above. Here's some recent examples of what I've written next to small talk:

- Their LinkedIn photo is outside of Gleneagles.
- We have the following mutual connections.
- We spoke three years ago.
- They're relatively new to the role.

Whatever I put is just a quick pointer for me to use if there's no obvious small talk to be had when the webcams connect. The Holy Grail is they appear and in the background they have a mountain bike, guitar or whatever, then you can abandon what you had in mind, and focus on that instead. You might wonder why you should pick a background object over a LinkedIn photo; well there's a reason the prospect has chosen to put it behind them and in your line of sight - they want you to ask about it! More importantly, they love talking about it.

In general though, small talk is overrated in sales; often it's confused with rapport building. They're two very different things. I try to keep small talk to a maximum of two minutes. This may not sound long but consider it this way; if the discovery call is 30 minutes long, then two minutes is 6.66% of your time. Seems crazy when you put it like that to spend any longer on it, doesn't it?

Unfortunately, I've seen far too many discovery calls start with over five minutes of small talk. This may be unhelpful talk centered on the weekend, the weather, hobbies, or whatever, each being discussed in such detail that the knock-on effect is huge. What ultimately happens is that the seller often runs out of time. This means they struggle to cover the prospect's current situation, needs, pain and personal motivation, and are thus unable to explain how they can potentially help and secure the next step.

Running out of time on a discovery call is a criminal offense. If you've not uncovered enough pain and "need" in the call to intrigue and excite the prospect, then they might not be willing to give you a second shot. In fairness to them, their time is their most precious asset, and if they're going to give more of it to you, a salesperson, then it needs to be for a good reason.

Here's the reality, no matter how good the small talk is, no matter how interested you were in their recent holiday, the small talk is not the reason they're going to buy from you.

Your prospects buy from you because you understand their compelling problems, along with their motivation and or need to solve them. The only way to do that is to uncover it, and that's what the focus of the discovery needs to be on - not the weather.

I'm not saying you shouldn't be pleasant and friendly. Just don't spend an age on it. The less time you spend on small talk, the more time you can spend on moving the needle.

Here's some transcripts of the openings of some of my discovery calls. Notice the lack of weather chat...

Example 1

Me: *"Hi Amy"*
Prospect: *"Hi Mark, how are you?"*
Me: *"I'm not too bad despite my hay fever playing up"*
Prospect: *"Oh no, you know, it must be bad at the moment, I'm struggling as well!"*
Me: *"It's a nightmare, how are you coping?"*
Prospect: *"Yeah, you know what it's like, my eyes are sore and I can't stop sneezing"*

Me: *"Ah, I feel for you"*

Prospect: *"Thanks, I do hate this time of year!"*

Me: *"I bet; hay fever aside, how's your morning been?"*

Prospect: *"it's been mayhem, I don't work Wednesdays, so Thursday mornings are always stressful, so apologies that I'm late!"*

Me: *"That's okay, is now still a good time?"*

Prospect: *"Yeah, it should be fine, it should be fine!"*

Me: *"Great, initially we had this call in for 30 minutes, but I'm curious, given your morning, how are you for time today?"*

Total length: 40 seconds.

Example 2

Me: *"Hi Kevin"*

Prospect: *"Hi Mark, are you alright?"*

Me: *"I'm very well thank you, yourself, how's your week been?"*

Prospect: *"Good yeah, just wrapping up the month; we had a really strong finish to the month so I'm really happy with that and, as of yesterday, we just delivered the company's best ever January, so I'm ecstatic with that - and we still have a few more days to go. What about yourself?"*

Me: *"Fantastic, yeah it's all pedal to the metal, all going well, so what's been your secret this month then?*

Prospect: *"To be fair, it's just a continuation of Q4 last year. I joined the company at the end of August and we had a strong end to the year. We did have a hiccup in December; that was a bit of a nightmare. But I think a lot of companies were in the same boat, so we focussed on pipeline and in January we hit the ground running. It's been hectic, so I put it down to pipeline to be fair Mark. As I say, we put a lot in December and now we're seeing the rewards so I'm really really happy with how it's going"*

Me: *"Fantastic, well I appreciate you sharing that with me and I'm glad you're having a great month. I know we rearranged this a few days ago due to a last-minute clash on your end; originally we did have this in for half an hour, but I'm curious, how are you for time today?"*

Total length: 1 minute 34 seconds.

Example 3

Prospect: *"Hi Mark"*
Me: *"Dan, how are you doing?"*
Prospect: *"I'm good; how are you?"*
Me: *"Yeah not too bad at all thanks, how's your week going so far?"*
Prospect: *"Good yeah, good, little bit quieter than last one. Sorry I had to postpone last-minute; it's been a hectic few weeks as we're in our final quarter for the*

year and lots of planning for our FY 23, which starts first of next month. So yeah, hard to find a break at the moment but this week's a bit quieter so I can get on with my admin and planning rather than spinning plates"

Me: *"Fantastic; well, I appreciate you're spinning a lot of plates, I suppose Dan, just to check because I know you have a little bit more time this week, but it still sounds like you're rammed. We have this for half an hour, but I'm curious, how are you for time this morning?"*

Total length: 52 seconds.

Quick tip: where you can, share something real and relatable with your prospect!

"Not too bad thanks, although I'm suffering quite badly from hay fever today".

"I just stepped on a plug; that aside I'm okay"

"I was alright until five minutes ago when my son threw his juice all over the floor"

These are just some of the ways I've responded when the prospect asks me *"how are you?"* Don't get me wrong; a lot of the time, like many people, I'll simply say *"I'm fine thanks"* and move on. However, if I have something to share that could be relevant or amusing, then I'll share it. I find it can be a great way to break the ice, as well as building empathy and humanising me; it can make the prospect feel like they're talking to a real person, not just another salesperson.

Example number one demonstrates this. Did you notice that although it was me who brought up hay fever, I managed to flip it and make it all about her? I asked how she was coping, I showed empathy, and she even shared her symptoms. All I said was that my hay fever was playing up.

Stuff like this can really help a prospect warm to you straight out the gate, as they can relate to everyday things. Stepping on plugs is the worst; parents know the frustration of juice being chucked about and fellow hay fever sufferers always connect over the misfortune of being allergic to pollen!

Step 3: Time Check

Confirming how long you have is important. Just because your call is in the calendar for half an hour, don't assume that's how long you actually have. Always check. You need to know how long you have. This is a step commonly missed out or mucked up by the sales professional. Allow me to explain; those who do check tend to ask in the following ways

"We have this in for 30 minutes, do you have a hard stop?"

"We have this in for 30 minutes, is that okay?"

Let me share why asking for the time in either of these ways could be clipping your calls short.

Firstly, when you ask *"...do you have a hard stop?"* the vast majority of the time, the best you'll get back is confirmation that they have the allotted time they initially agreed to i.e. *"Yeah, that's fine"* or *"Yeah, I've got the time blocked out; we're good"*.

When you ask, *"We have this in for 30 minutes, is that okay?"* you're practically inviting the prospect to cut you short; that's where you get responses like:

"Actually, I do have another call and could do with some time to prepare; could we do this in 20 minutes?"

or

"If we could do this quicker, that would be great"

Immediately, this is the prospect taking control of the call and that means you're losing grip and working to their pace. It doesn't make for a good start.

Here's an alternative way to ask. It's a subtle switch, but I've used this on hundreds of discovery calls:

"We have this in for 30 minutes, but I know things can change - just so I understand, when you look at your calendar, how are you for time today?"

As I say, I've asked it specifically this way on hundreds of discovery calls, and while this isn't bullet proof, it's common to see the prospect's eyes shift as they look at their calendar to check their availability and then I often get responses like:

"I've got the half hour and if we need a little more time, I'm okay with that"

"Yep, all good; my next meeting isn't until 12, so we can run over."

"Yeah, I'm fine I've not got anything after this either so we're all good"

Bingo. Now you know, *if* you need it, there's more time to play with.

My advice here though is that, if you do need the extra time, still check with the prospect. For example, at the 25-minute mark, say something like this:

"I know you said we can run over; just to check, could we take ten more minutes now and that'll ensure we cover everything we need and set us up nicely for the demo?"

Step 4: Agenda

This step is key. The delivery and content of the agenda can make or break your discovery call.

You have to get it right.

Understandably, many people refer to the agenda as an "upfront contract" (a Sandler term) because that's what you're doing - you're laying out your plan for the call and getting the prospect to agree to it.

If you can get them to agree to your plan, you're in full control; the tempo is set, and expectations managed.

My agenda sounds like this

"Mrs Prospect, tell me what you think about this as a plan of action...

I'll start with a quick recap of how we got here, followed by what piqued your interest and what you'd like to get from the conversation to make this a good investment of your time.

Depending on what you'd like to get from this conversation, I'll probably need to ask a few questions so I can better understand your needs. I'll then share some relevant ideas with you, ideas you may or may not have considered.

As two sales professionals, what we're working towards is one of two outcomes; and, come the end of the call you'll be able to decide what outcome that is.

Outcome one, being you say "Thanks for your time, but this isn't for me" - and that's totally fine. In fact, feel free to tell me at any point if you don't feel like this is for you and I'll do the same.

Let's think positively though and imagine we get to outcome two, that being that we get to the end of this call and you're excited and wanting to learn more. In which case, what we'll do is compare calendars and schedule in the next steps, which is typically an online demo...

Does that sound like a fair plan of action to you?"

Let me break down why this style of agenda/upfront agreement works piece by piece...

"Mrs Prospect, tell me what you think about this as a plan of action"

The phrase "plan of action" is carefully considered. It's a commanding phrase, and it subtly tells the prospect that there is a clear plan, and that you're leading this call. People in general feel more comfortable when they know there's a plan in place.

"I'll start with a quick recap of how we got here"

I tell them I'll start with a quick recap because I want them to know that, after the agenda I'm going to be the one to speak first. It's my recap; I'm in control; I'm running the conversation.

Why? After you've given the agenda it's important you take control of the conversation. If you don't, then you run the risk of the prospect going off on a tangent and them telling you what they think you want to hear. I've seen this happen plenty of times. The prospect takes the mic and starts to talk about the company history, their career to date and so on; and it just gobbles up a big chunk of your time.

To avoid this, you need to point your prospect in the right direction by focusing them on what you're here to talk about and starting the discovery with a recap. Explaining "how we got here" enables you to do that. In this recap, you are able to remind them of the initial outreach and the reason they took the call in the first place. This gets them focussed and ready to talk about what you want to cover.

If this was an inbound lead, you should tweak it to, *"It would be good to start with the reasons for you booking the call"* - more on this in Chapter 5, on the Golden Minute.

"...followed by what piqued your interest and what you'd like to get from the conversation to make this a good investment of your time"

This is important, as you're telling them that you want to understand why they're interested and that this is a conversation, not a sales pitch. You want to understand what they want to get from their time investment. It's subtle, yet it tells them this is a consultative conversation where you have their best interests at heart.

If this is an inbound lead, you can remove the start of this sentence as it's covered by asking the reasons as to why they booked the call. Instead, you can use the line *"...what you'd like to get from the conversation to make this a good investment of your time"*

"...depending on what you'd like to get from this conversation, I'll probably need to ask a few questions so I can better understand your needs. I'll then share some relevant ideas with you, ideas you may or may not have considered"

This sentence sets expectations by explaining that you'll be asking them questions (with justification behind them), therefore getting them into the mindset that this is a discovery call. They're now better prepared mentally to answer your questions and they're more likely to be compliant as they know this means you'll be more relevant with your ideas.

The "may or may not have considered" is your way of sounding detached from the outcome. It's the opposite of what they expect to hear from a sales professional. Prospects expect the seller to believe everyone should buy their product/service. Therefore, by telling them they may or may not have considered your ideas, you reduce any feeling of pressure.

...*"as two sales professionals"*

This line can be removed or adapted to simply "as two professionals". I like it, and encourage you to keep it in your agenda because it adds empathy (one professional to another), familiarity (people like people like themselves), and humanisation ("we walk in each other's shoes").

"...what we're working towards is one of two outcomes; and, come the end of the call you'll be able to decide what outcome that is"

This sets the expectation and purpose of the call. Everything we discuss is leading us towards one of two outcomes that may come at the end of the call; it's *their* decision. This again detaches you from the outcome and reduces the feeling of pressure a prospect can feel. Yet we're also saying "we're working towards", making it feel like this is a conversation between two equals. We're in this together, therefore let's work as a cohesive unit to get you to a place where you can decide what you want to do next. It nicely implies teamwork, without them feeling like they're being sold to.

"Outcome one, being you say thanks for your time, but this isn't for me - and that's totally fine. In fact, feel free to tell me at any point if

you don't feel like this is for you and I'll do the same"

This again is us telling the prospect we're not attached to the outcome and we don't mind if this isn't a fit. It's another soundbite they're just not expecting to hear from a seller. If you use this line and you're on a video call, you'll notice how often a prospect smiles when they hear you say this. It's a smile of relief. They feel relaxed knowing that you'll be okay with this call ending in "No". Sharing this potential outcome lowers the prospect's barriers. It's so powerful.

"Let's think positively though and imagine we get to outcome two, that being that we get to the end of this call and you're excited and wanting to learn more. In which case, what we'll do is compare calendars and schedule in the next steps, which is typically an online demo..."

Telling someone to think positively does just that, it encourages positivity. This outcome tells them that if this call goes well, there is a next step, and that it isn't anything scary - there's no order forms or asking for credit card details. Instead, it's simply comparing calendars to book in a demo. It also subtly tells them not to expect to see anything on this call.

Quick tip: Did you notice I put the (potential) negative outcome first?

Whenever I coach discovery calls where the sales professional gives an agenda with two outcomes, they typically put the positive outcome first, followed by the negative, and it drives me up the wall. Why end your agenda on a negative note? Put the potential negative outcome first, then finish your agenda with the potential positive outcome! This also sounds far less self-serving to the prospect.

"...does that sound like a fair plan of action to you?"

This is when you get their commitment to your agenda and they verbally sign the upfront agreement.

The word "fair" is carefully chosen. In general, people see the word in a positive light, as everyone likes to be seen to be fair.

You then end the agenda by reinforcing the "plan of action", and the fact that it's your plan, and you're in control.

How do you tell if your agenda worked? They verbally agree and then go quiet. They're waiting for you to give the recap you promised.

If you find your prospects regularly start to speak after you've delivered your agenda, I'd encourage you to go back and listen to the recording. When listening back, be honest with yourself. Were you confident with the delivery? Often, when a prospect takes control after the agenda, it's because they've sensed a lack of confidence or ownership and they dive in to take control. This can be particularly true when dealing with assertive prospects.

Of course you can deliver a great agenda after which the prospect still tries to take control. It's just in some people's nature. But you can still rescue it, and here's a transcript of me doing just that:

Agenda delivered

Prospect: *"Okay, let me start by telling you what we do, and what I want to talk about today"*
Mark: *"Yep, it makes sense to cover that; however let's make sure we don't leave any stones unturned. Let's start from the beginning; let's go over how we got here first and take it from there. Does that sound fair?"*
Prospect: *"Absolutely, of course"*

I was then back in control.

Had I not taken the control back, it's easy to imagine (and I've seen it happen all too many times before) I would have sat listening to five minutes or longer of the prospect sharing information that wouldn't help me move the needle. The time lost here, along with the small talk and time check, could easily have seen me lose ten minutes of my 30-minute call - 33% of my time!

When you lose the control in sales, you typically lose the sale!

So there you have it, your step-by-step guide to delivering a solid agenda and setting the tone for a great discovery call.

Chapter Five

The Golden Minute

So you've delivered your agenda; now what?

We need to get our prospect to open up about their problems, fast. The first question is key. If we can immediately unlock the prospect and get them to open up, we're off to a great start.

When a prospect "spills the beans" at the start of the call, I refer to it as the "golden minute"; in this case, as the seller, you must pay close attention to what they're saying and how they're saying it.

The first question you'll ask post-agenda will depend on the source of the meeting: this may be:

- Booked by someone else such as an SDR/BDR.
- Self-generated.
- Inbound.
- Referral.
- Returning lead.

Let's look at the perfect play for each scenario

Booked by Someone Else

Once you've delivered your agenda, give the prospect a quick recap as to how you got here; this is important because the initial conversation wasn't with you; without this recap you'd be naively expecting the prospect to have crystal clear memory as to what convinced them to agree to the discovery call in the first place.

Here's a couple of transcripts of my "recaps" when an SDR has booked the meeting for me

"So in terms of how we got here, James - you spoke with my colleague Nia at the end of last month and you kindly said you were happy to hear her out as you managed SDRs who cold-called yourself; and while that's a nice thing to say, I'm guessing something that Nia said must have piqued your interest

On the call she led with two problems that people in sales leadership roles can encounter

The first problem being that while their sales team performs okay to targets... every quarter it just feels like it's harder than it should be to hit the collective revenue goal. As the manager, you know the team is capable of more, but the uncomfortable truth is that the team is simply lacking some required skills to be truly successful.

And it's hard; you know you can help develop them, yet you spin so many plates as it is, finding the time to coach each person 1:1 on a weekly basis feels impossible. The result? You stay stuck on the hamster wheel. Unable to get off. The problem never truly fixes itself and the team stagnates. Some leave for better opportunities, others stay and regress, and others fail in the role altogether. Either way, the team is unlikely to fulfill their potential and overachieve on the business plans, which stifles commission, bonuses and further career opportunities for you as their manager.

The second problem is similar, however they do find the time to give each person in their team the 1:1 coaching they need to be successful. Yet, despite the time constantly invested in coaching it's simply not having the desired impact as quickly as required and, at the end of each quarter when the revenue is counted they're left frustrated as the leader of the team and unsure what to do to truly improve and develop their team to hit and exceed revenue goals.

I'm just curious out of those two things James, you've just joined the company and no doubt have been set objectives to achieve beyond 'the number'; what parts from Nia's message resonated with you?"

Here's what followed

Prospect: *"It was the first one, definitely"*
Me: *"Right; okay, tell me more"*

James then spoke for two and a half minutes about the problem, why it piqued their interest and how it resonated - this is what I'm referring to as the golden minute.

In this dialogue, it's them speaking all about the problem and why it resonated. I get to hear first-hand the problem(s) in their own words.

It's critical you're paying attention to their tone, energy, emphasis and words used; all of this is key information.

Your active listening is crucial at this stage. You must focus on what they're saying and how they're saying it instead of thinking about your next question. Everything you learn here will prove helpful in the remainder of the call (and beyond) with your prospect.

Let me further break down this transcript and explain why I said what I said:

Firstly it's not uncommon for the prospect to tell me they took the meeting simply because my SDR "did a great job" with their outreach - as nice as that is, it's not helpful to me in finding pain so I took that "reason" away from them, I acknowledge it and moved it on by saying, "...*while that's a nice thing to say, I'm guessing something that Nia said must have piqued your interest*"

I then re-share the problems from the cold call - except this time, I expanded on them. If you've read our first book, '*Problem Prospecting?!*' you'll notice the problems here are quite lengthy in comparison to the cold call - that's intentional. I have more time here - more time to make them land and get them leaning in to learn more.

I also want you to notice how the problems follow a pattern of using a "trigger word" a problem and an outcome of that problem'

Trigger words are emotional words like: uncomfortable, worried, frustrated, annoyed, confused and so on. They are used to evoke a particular feeling in your prospect.

Let's look again at first problem from the transcript below; this time I'll <u>underline the trigger word</u>, **bold the problem** and **<u>bold + underline the outcome</u>** so you can see exactly what I was doing

*The first problem being that while their sales team performs <u>okay</u> to targets...every quarter it just feels like it's <u>harder</u> than it should be to **hit the collective revenue goal**. As the manager you know the team is capable of more but the <u>uncomfortable truth</u> is the team is simply **lacking some required skills to be truly successful.***

And it's hard, you know you can help develop them yet you spin so many plates as it is, finding the time to coach each person 1:1 on a weekly basis feels <u>impossible</u>. The result? ***You stay stuck on the hamster wheel. Unable to get off.*** *The problem never truly fixes itself and the team <u>stagnates</u>.* ***Some leave for better opportunities, others stay and regress, and others fail in the role altogether.*** *Either way,* ***<u>the team is unlikely to fulfil their potential and overachieve on the business plans, which stifles commission, bonuses and further career opportunities for them and you as their manager.</u>***

Once I've reiterated the problems, I link it back to my prospect and their goals.

In this example I did this by first referencing that they've just joined the company and then saying, "*...and no doubt have been set objectives to achieve beyond 'the number'.*"

Notice I've included "beyond the number" as the number is always the main goal of a sales leader. By referencing and downplaying the obvious goal, I'm giving a subtle nod to the idea that I know their world, which encourages them to think beyond the obvious.

I then asked James directly, *"what parts from Nia's message resonated with you?"* and then went silent, patiently awaiting the golden minute.

Quick tip: prospects new to the role are one of my favorite types to have. When someone is new to a role (promoted or newly hired) they're typically optimistic, excited, and keen to make changes and show their employer what they're capable of. All you have to do is work out how solving the problem ties back to what they're being measured on. I subtly mention that in this example by saying *"you've just joined the company and no doubt have been set objectives to achieve"* which will put their remit upon taking the job back to the front of their mind.

Prospects who are new to the role of company do however come with a warning; as they're new they might not know how to actually buy within this business - though, having said that, this can be true of people that have been in the role a long time as well!

Here's another transcript from when my SDR, George had booked a call for me

"So, Molly let me recap as to how we got here, my colleague George gave you a call and mentioned a couple of problems people in your role typically face

The first problem is they know that to get their reps hitting the goals they've set for them, coaching is the number one thing they should be doing as their manager. Here's the problem; despite the best will in the world, managers have got a million and one other things to be doing - and therefore they don't have the time to sit with their teams on a 1:1 basis and coach them consistently - the time they do get together is instead all about 'the number' and metrics.

The other challenge is the dynamics of being a boss and a coach; salespeople can be struggling and yet they don't feel like they can admit to their boss they have skills gaps, because being vulnerable with their boss is too uncomfortable, meaning they continue to try to be successful without seeking the help they need

And the third thing George mentioned was how lots of companies have personal development budgets sitting there and yet reps aren't using it, they've got..."

Prospect *interrupts me mid-sentence*: *"YEP, that's exactly what I'm facing, right... So there's a budget there for development; it's just not being used, which is why I was curious to understand what you can do"*

Me: *"Perfect, yeah; so that was the third challenge. Interestingly, when you spoke to George, you actually said all three were relevant and, of course, anything since that call to now could have changed... so to clarify, out of those three things*

- *Lack of time.*
- *Reps and the dynamic of having a manager as their coach.*

- *And that personal development budget.*

What was it that piqued your interest the most?

Prospect: *"Probably all three, I'd say number two is the least prioritised right now but one and three certainly; and what's come to light more recently is some skills gaps across the team, particularly around negotiation. So I'd love to hear how you could help coach our team to be better at negotiation"*

Me: *Sure, and we can talk through that then; just so I understand, help bring that to life for me. Can you tell me more about that?*

I then got two minutes of the prospect sharing how the team were poor negotiators, who discounted too quickly and too easily, without getting anything in return and the impact it's having on his ability to get the team to target. The golden minute.

This transcript is very similar to the previous one. However there was a key moment that shows the importance of listening back to initial outreach and recording your team's calls. The prospect interrupted to eagerly tell me it was problem number 3. It would have been easy for me to get excited at hearing the prospect tell me this and then focus the whole discovery on that.

Instead (and because I knew the prospect has shared other problems in the original cold call), I recapped all three problems and asked my question: *"...what was it that piqued your interest the most?"* and then it reset my prospects' mind and we unlocked the first problem. This turned out to be a specific business problem - her sales team being poor at negotiation and needing help.

I then got the golden minute by asking for more details: *"... just so I understand, help bring that to life for me, can you tell me more about that?"*

So here are the key takeaways for when the meeting is booked for you by someone else

- Listen back to the cold call recording or read the email/LinkedIn exchange.
- Don't assume they'll recall their reason for taking the call in the first place.
- Focus the prospect on the problems, not the quality of the outreach by recapping the problems discussed
  - ☐ Rephrase/expand on them if you need to, with the following formula (trigger words + problems + outcomes)
- Get the golden minute by asking them to elaborate on the reasons it piqued their interest and go silent.
- Actively listen to what they say and how they say it, making note of specific words and phrases used.

Quick tip: if you're finding "no shows" a problem when the meeting is booked for you by someone else, read Chapter Thirteen in our previous book, '***Problem Prospecting?!***' for actionable tips and tricks

Self-Generated

The playbook for self-generated discovery calls is somewhat similar, in the sense that you'll need to remind them of your initial outreach; but I find you can bring a bit more personality and humor to it. After all, they're on the discovery call as a result of your outreach.

Here's a transcript of the start of a discovery with someone I had initially cold called myself.

Me: *"So Tariq, I gave you a cold call on a Friday afternoon and caught you in the middle of having a cup of tea and a biscuit"*

Tariq: *"I remember, I remember that ha."*

Me: *"You may recall I led with a couple of problems that sometimes resonate with enablement leaders like you ...*

The first is that they know their front line sellers are being let down because they're not getting the development and coaching they need from their managers to enable them to hit their revenue goals. There can be reasons for this of course; the manager might lack the necessary skill to be an effective coach. Often though they simply don't have the time to regularly give each person in their team the 1:1 coaching they need.

The other thing I shared was that enablement leaders can take it upon themselves to deliver effective training but they know that, without the regular coaching to reinforce it, most of the training is quickly forgotten and not put into practice, meaning the development and improvement in the front line sales team isn't great enough to drive the performance of the team to the required level, as a result company revenue goals are missed.

I also briefly mentioned that some companies give personal development budgets but they're disappointed with how often it goes unused by their front line sellers

It felt like you agreed with everything I was saying, but the thing that we spoke most about on our initial call was the front line managers not having the time or skill to coach... now I've recapped, it would be helpful to hear from you. What was it about that problem that made you want to spend time with me today?"

My prospect (Tariq) then opened up about the problem and why what I said had resonated; you can see that represented in the graphic below.

Mark Ackers

Them

To explain this image further, these are two talk bars - mine and Tariq's. The blocks on each line indicate when that person is talking.

The talk bars show a bit of small talk at the start between Tariq and me. Then I start to talk, I give my agenda and then go into the start of the call as documented in the transcript above, you can see the small line on Tariq's talk bar (labeled as 'Them') where he said *"I remember, I remember that ha"*

Once I'd finished speaking and paused for the golden minute, Tariq delivered; he actually spoke for 2 minutes and 54 seconds. For context, the discovery call lasted 30 minutes and 42 seconds so this golden minute actually represents a massive 9.44% of the conversation.

As you can see, it's a very similar play to when a meeting has been booked by someone else. The only real difference is that I can reference the cold call in a more personal way.

Quick tip: always make note of anything the prospect says in the cold call and use it in the next call. It brings familiarity and trust as their brain feels more relaxed, they feel like they know you, as you've spoken before so you're not a stranger.

I've called people before and they've been in the gym, out at lunch, or even the classic "I'm in a meeting and thought you were someone else" - whatever it is, no matter how small (like in this example of Tariq having a cup of tea), reference it and relax them.

The key takeaways are similar to a call that was booked by someone else; just remember to use whatever nuggets you've taken from the initial outreach to make you feel more 'familiar' to the prospect.

Inbound

Inbound calls are different; there's a level of intent from the prospect and we need to know what that level is. For example, are they just curious, ready to buy or somewhere in between?

Either way, we need to find out the reason they wanted to speak and their level of intent, fast!

This is my playbook for starting my discovery calls with an inbound opportunity

- Small talk.
- Time check (which sounds like this - *"typically, when you book a call through the website it gives you a standard 30-minute slot but, just so I understand, when you look at your calendar, how are you for time today?"*)

And then this

"Mrs Prospect, tell me what you think about this as a plan of action...

Let's start with the reasons you've booked a call and what you'd like to cover - depending on what you say I'll no doubt need to ask a few questions so I can better understand your needs and we can take it from there, does that sound like a fair plan of action to you?"

The delivery is nice and quick.

From there, once they agree to your "plan of action" here's only one question to ask

"Help me understand, what's the reason we're talking today?"

Ask that question, in that way, and you'll get your golden minute.

Quick tip: Notice I avoid the word "why" - as in "why are we speaking today" - This may seem innocuous. but it can trigger a person to feel like they need to justify their actions. So make a simple swap to "what's the reason" instead. Chris Voss taught me that.

You may also get some information shared in advance by a prospect. For example, when you book a call with MySalesCoach, we say, "Please share anything that will help prepare for our meeting" on the booking form. It's an optional field, and approximately 60% of the time, the prospect leaves notes that help us.

I will always reference what's been said, but I also encourage them to expand upon it; here's an example of me doing that

This was the message left on the form by my prospect, Simon.

Please share anything that will help prepare for our meeting:

I manage a global team of SDRs, AEs, and CSMs. We previously worked with a training provider, but the contract was not renewed. I'm now exploring the idea of 1:1 coaching for my team and would like to understand your approach, offering, and pricing.

I start the discovery call in my normal way

- Small talk (it turns out that Simon, like me, was from Essex, which always helps.)
- Time check.
- Agenda.

This is followed immediately by

"So, Simon, when you booked the call in with MySalesCoach, you left a note that said you have a global team of SDRs, AEs and CSMs and that you've been working with a training provider but decided not to continue working with them and that you were interested in the idea of 1:1 coaching for your sales and customer success team

Help me understand that a little better; take me back to the moment you booked the call. I'm guessing something happened that day for you to go onto Google, find us and book a call. What happened?"

You can see how the start of the call played out in the image below

Mark Ackers

Them

With us both hailing from the same glorious county, there was more small talk than usual and it was quite back and forth - I then delivered my agenda followed by the above transcript. At the point where I stop talking we're 2 minutes and 47 seconds into a 34 minute and 12 second discovery call (8.13%).

Once I ask, *"What happened that day that led to you booking a call with us,"* the golden minute commences with Simon speaking for a long period, uninterrupted - he spoke for 3 minutes and 37 seconds (10.5% of the entire discovery call) giving me so much detail and context.

The reason I went down this path is because I wanted to let Simon know I'd read and understood his reasons for booking the call, but I wanted a deeper understanding, I therefore transported him back to the moment he booked the call, I want to understand essentially "why now?" What made him think, 'It's time to solve this problem' and take action by booking a call with MySalesCoach. It's easy to imagine that, if I had just ignored his message and asked, *"What's the reason we're talking today?"* I'd have just gotten the same message and Simon would have been frustrated as it would have felt like he wasted his time leaving the message in the first place and he'd potentially doubt me as a professional.

Referral - From a Friend

My face lights up when I see an inbound call that's the result of a referral, or when, at the start of the call, the prospect says, *"My friend said I should take a look"*.

When coaching discovery calls, my heart sinks if "the gift" of a referral is wasted, as it often is - and thats such an error.

Average salespeople will acknowledge it and ask "who" made the referral but that's about it. In fact, let me give you an example; this time I'm the prospect and I was referred to the business.

When booking the discovery call with this company (who shall remain nameless), I left the following message

"Hello, I'm looking to see how [company name] can help me and my team as I feel like your product could help us and I've heard good things about your product from a friend."

Salesperson: *"Do you mind letting me know who it was that recommended us so I can thank them"*

Me, the prospect: *"Yeah sure, it was my friend, Steve at [company name] I know he's been a customer for a while now and he loves it."*

Salesperson: *"Brilliant; yeah I know Steve, I'll drop him a message and thank him. It's always nice when people recommend us; that's how you get the best business. We're looking to grow and people like Steve recommending us will help us do that very quickly."*

I don't want to sound too harsh, but that is shocking from the salesperson. It was a total waste of "the gift".

If I was the salesperson in this instance, here what I'd say to the prospect

"You mentioned that your friend, Steve recommended us - tell me more"

That question/instruction alone could be all you need to say; the phrase 'tell me more' can open a prospect up and result in them telling you everything.

Quick tip: When your prospect stops talking, just hang on and keep quiet for 2 seconds. It's not an easy feat, however, when you master this and keep quiet at the end of their sentence you'll be amazed at how many prospects fill the silence by "reloading" and begin speaking again, giving you even more information.

Other questions to have in your playbook when a referral is made.

- Out of interest, what's the context that led to your friend suggesting you speak with us?
- Did your friend explain their reasons for choosing to work with us?
- Did they share the results they've seen since working with us?
- Help me understand, how much does their situation and the results they were looking for (and have now achieved) reflect YOUR situation?
- Given you've heard good things about us from someone you know and trust, what would be your concerns about working with us?

Referrals from happy customers typically close at a much higher rate than any other lead. So, focussing the start of the discovery call on the referral and understanding the reason the two were speaking and why your company was brought up as a viable solution is like a shortcut to pain.

Referral From a Boss/Colleague

Again, when a prospect has been referred to you, you start your discovery call in a good place. You have an advantage in that the prospect either takes this seriously because their boss has told them to speak with you or you have social proof, as their colleague has suggested you speak.

Let's start with the top down referral. The boss has told them to speak to you. Often they've suggested this because this person would be the one who would directly use your product or service.

While it's a powerful referral, it can be wasted if you don't use it effectively. To do that you need to understand their reasons for making the referral and replay that to your new contact. You also need to understand their bosses' emotion(s) about the referral. Therefore you need to get crystal clear on what business problem the boss is trying to solve (which they've probably tasked their subordinate to solve) and how they believe your product/service will help them achieve that.

Once you understand that, you can effectively bring the situation to life after your agenda and get your prospect to open up.

Here's an example where I've done just that.

For context, I'd had a 20 minute conversation with a Vice President of Sales called Duncan and he'd told me to speak with his Sales Director, James, as it was his team that needed our services.

I started the discovery call with James in the same way: a bit of small talk (he was a new father so that was easy enough), time check, and agenda. Then I said this:

"So as you'll know, I had a good conversation with Duncan and he mentioned that your team needed coaching. He said you had a team of five sales professionals each at different stages in their career. Duncan explained that there's a number of key sales skills lacking across the team

which is impacting performance and that, despite you having all the will in the world to coach and develop them, you're simply stretched too thin already - coaching to address these skills gaps just isn't happening. The impact? Every quarter you and the team stay on the hamster wheel, trying to hit the targets, but it's frustrating as it's been the same story for a while. It's got to the point where you need to develop and upskill the team in order to help them be successful.

I guess a good place to start would be, how accurate is Duncan with that?"

When I asked that question, the discovery call was 5 minutes and 48 seconds in; you can see in the image below just how much James then opened up about his current situation. He spoke for 3 minutes and 15 seconds uninterrupted.

FYI: The transcript above is labeled "How we got here" in the following image, in the graph, the "'sorry'" is where James apologised about rearranging the call.

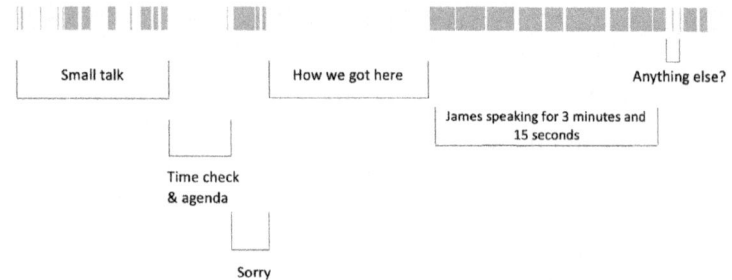

At the end of his answer (to *"How accurate is Duncan with that?"*), James said:

"We have a desire to fix this challenge; how we fix that challenge probably isn't decided yet but it's definitely worthwhile having this conversation to learn about what you do, and see how that can fit into the mix basically"

Despite having a lengthy 3 minute and 15 second answer I knew there was more information to be gathered so, once James had finished speaking I asked one of my favorite questions to ask after the golden minute.

"Is there anything else you think I need to know?"

I then got another 50 seconds of information as shown in the image. That's just over 4 minutes of information. Another 643 words.

Let me explain why I said what I said by breaking it down into sections

"So as you'll know, I had a good conversation with Duncan..."

I'm just reinforcing the fact that I've spoken with his boss and the conversation was positive - subtly telling him his boss is onside.

"...and he mentioned that your team needed coaching, he said you had a team of five sales professionals each at different stages in their career. "

This is me reinforcing that his senior wants his team to be coached; this makes it very difficult for him to tell me they don't. I'm also sharing information to show I'm "in the know", and aware of the situation, making me sound more consultative and already on the inside. *"Duncan explained that there's a number of key sales skills lacking across the team which is impacting performance and that despite you having all the will in the world to coach and develop them, you're simply stretched too thin already - coaching to address these skills gaps just isn't happening. "*

I continue to double down on this, by further explaining what Duncan told me. I use the phrase "key sales skills" to acknowledge that this is important. I then move on to the impact of this problem by stating it's "impacting performance".

The next bit is key, I don't want James to be defensive and push back, so I make it "okay" to admit to this problem and the impact it's having by telling him that his boss already knows he's stretched too thin - despite having the will. This makes it feel "okay" to admit to the problem, it's almost not his fault anymore, and his boss knows about it.

"The impact? Every quarter you and the team stay on the hamster wheel, trying to hit the targets, but it's frustrating as it's been the same story for a while. It's got to the point where you need to develop and upskill the team in order to help them be successful."

I'm now turning the screw on the impact, trying to make him feel emotional and frustrated with the situation, using the hamster wheel analogy, labeling how it must feel (frustrating), and saying that it's been like this for a while. This means it has reached the point where something needs to change - again all with the backdrop that this has been discussed with his boss, Duncan. All James needs to do is admit to me this is right, and then he can't go back on it; these words now become his words and his state of play.

"I guess a good place to start would be, how accurate is Duncan with that?"

And this is where I get him to do just that, tell me his boss is right, tell me this is the problem, this is the impact of that problem, it's been like this for a while, now is the time to fix it AND, most importantly, he doesn't have the time to do it.

Returning Prospect

We all have those prospects that fall off the face of the Earth. They ghost us. Is it just me, or do we sometimes convince ourselves they must have died? Well, some prospects do come back from the dead...

When a prospect returns, it's really easy for us to get excited. *They're back! They must want to buy.*

Personally, I don't get excited when a prospect returns. In fact, I feel quite the opposite. Why? This prospect in the past has caused me a myriad of frustration, anxiety and maybe even embarrassment with my manager. This prospect would have had me in "chase mode" and ultimately they've wasted my time. They've also shown that they can and will ghost me at their convenience, and that means they've got it in them to do it again. Moreover, in my experience they're more likely to ghost you again than buy from you - when you think of it like that, why would you greet them with open arms?

When a prospect returns, you need to be skeptical, not excited. The number one thing we need to do is figure out why they want to speak again and what's different this time round.

Before we get into that, let me share some examples of prospects returning from the grave.

Example 1: My prospect and I had a few calls, a proposal was requested and sent over. And I then unexpectedly entered Ghost town.

After several attempts I sent my last message (below) on the 28th Feb 2023

FEB 28, 2023

Mark Ackers 🔗 · 2:38 PM

Hey ▪▪▪▪ little nudge from me..

How are you on the morning of the 15th or 17th (after 10am)?

Let me know and I'll ping an invite over,

Mark

No reply.

Well, not at first. 614 days later I received this:

FEB 28, 2023

Mark Ackers 🔗 · 2:38 PM

Hey ███ little nudge from me..

How are you on the morning of the 15th or 17th (after 10am)?

Let me know and I'll ping an invite over,

Mark ✔

NOV 3, 2024

███████████ 🔗 · 10:55 AM

Hi Mark .....are you free for 30 mins on Wednesday to talk through your offering and how that might be embedded into ███████ for next year?

Example number 2: This prospect has tried to buy from me twice in the past; we agreed on the 25th of June 2024 that it was time to close the file and part as friends.

202 days later I got a text out of the blue.

Mon, 13 Jan at 16:28

Hi Mark, I've got a starting budget of ████ for my own coaching. Key is to understand messaging and what is or isn't working for us and how we could best address that. Look forward to hearing from you and if you need anything else then let me know. Thanks, ██████

Example number 3: This prospect has had me jump through a few hoops before and ultimately decided it wasn't for them, so imagine my surprise when I get the email below nine months later:

I could share many more examples, but you get my point.

What you have also probably noticed is how unphased they seem to be, almost oblivious to the fact that, in the past we'd had a number of conversations, possibly sent a proposal and they had just ghosted me. They didn't answer calls, they didn't reply to messages, nothing and then, when they want something, they act dead casual. It's like they expect you to be thrilled to hear from them. It's a power dynamic. *I'm the buyer, you will be happy to hear from me. You will serve me.*

Personal Dev » Inbox ×

✦ Summarise this email

to me ▾

Opens: 1   Log email to HubSpot ▾

Hi Mark,

I need help getting my guys to use their personal development.

I'm looking to build a menu of options for them, almost forcing them to pick one of three.

I would like to include MySalesCoach as one of those options.

How can I make this work? How can I make it possible for them to get on and do something?

Thanks

--

Head of Sales

So, you need to take control back, but before you do that, get them on the call.

My replies to these kinds of messages are typically pretty casual, my aim is to just get them on a call and take it from there. The replies are typically something like this:

"Sounds interesting, let's have a chat and see where it takes us."

If their message is a little elusive, I'll slip in a question and set the expectation that I'm wanting more information when we next speak.

"Interesting, I did not expect to hear from you - let's have a chat and you can tell me a little more"

What I'm ultimately doing is avoiding friction in a text format. Email, LinkedIn, text messages and so on all have the potential for your message to be read in a way you never intended. Just get them on the call and, from there, you can suss them out.

Once you're on the call, avoid phrases like:
- "It's so good to hear from you."
- "This is a pleasant surprise."
- "You getting back in touch has made my day."

Yes, they're all me being a bit sarcastic, but the sentiment is true; don't act delighted to be speaking with them. Be polite, of course, but be suspicious. Think "suspect" not prospect.

Here's a recent transcript where I did that - for context we'd met at an event, and agreed to speak again, then they had cancelled the call and never replied when I tried to rearrange. Four months later they messaged me asking to speak.

Prospect: *"Hi, Mark, can you hear me okay?"*
Me: *"Christine, I can, how are you?"*
Prospect: *"I am well, sorry. My camera today has been really glitchy on me. I'm not sure what's going on. Hopefully, it settles down, so sorry."*
Me: *"Oh, that's okay, the camera seems to be working fine. It's good to get to speak to you. I must admit I didn't think we were going to speak again..."*
Prospect: *"Oh no, really? Oh, gosh, no, not at all, Mark. I'm sorry. You know what's happened to me? We've had a lot of changes in our business and everything so it's something that I just put on the back burner. I am really sorry, Mark, I'm sorry that I made you feel that way. It was always my intention to come back to you and now I need you more than you could ever know."*
Me: *"I appreciate you sharing your reasons, I didn't take it personally, so it's all good. I assume something changed."*

Now I know what you're thinking, that seems like a really nice prospect, and she was. Here's another transcript:

The context here is that Dylan (the prospect) and I met at an event (the Sales Innovation Expo), at the back end of 2023, then we had a couple of positive calls. We built what we both felt was a good business case to work together, and, frustratingly, his CEO put the blockers on the whole thing. I never really got an explanation as to why. It just went all quiet. Eight months later, Dylan emailed me asking if we could speak.

Prospect: *"Hey Mark"*
Me: *"Dylan. Hello! How are you doing?*
Prospect: *"Yeah, good. You?"*
Me: *"Not too bad. Thanks. What's been happening?"*
Prospect: *"It's manic here, manic manic manic."*
Me: *"In a good way?"*
Prospect: *"Yeah, we probably doubled in size since we last spoke, so a lot of moving parts, even more than before."*
Me: *"That all sounds good. I mean, I appreciate that will come with stress. But that sounds good. It sounds like business must be doing well then?"*

Dylan then spends 29 seconds talking, uninterrupted about company expansion beyond just sales, highlighting challenges in accessing developers and legal teams, the recent establishment of an operations team, and overall growth into multiple new teams rather than just scaling one department rapidly.

Me: *"It sounds like you have been busy since we last spoke; that was January by the way - which surprised me. It feels like it was longer"*

Prospect: *"Yeah, it's been full on, adding new teams, and new people. We had to get a 3rd office. We've outgrown the first. January... God was it really? Yeah it has been a while!"*

Me: *"indeed..."*

Slight intentional pause from me - thing is, while the pause is needed to shift the conversation from small talk to discovery, I know I need to speak first, so while I'm intentionally pausing, I'm watching my prospect intently. If I feel he's about to speak, I'll kill the pause, and speak before him. I want to control the next part of the call and set the tone.

Me: *"I know you'll take this the way it's intended... When I saw your email asking if we could speak, my gut reaction was 'urgh, really?' and I don't think my reaction will surprise you because we've danced this dance before, we had what we both felt was a solid business case and it got to the CEO and he said no, for reasons that you've never really shared either...*

Then I thought to myself, okay, maybe this is interesting what's the reason he's come back, where did it go wrong last time, what's changed and why does he want to speak now - so yeah, I'm really curious to know, what's the reason we're speaking again and has anything really changed that'll stop us from getting the same outcome as last time?"

I then got a 93 second monologue, 375 words in total, where Dylan explained why the CEO had said no the previous time, the pain they've had by not offering our coaching services to their sales reps and why MySalesCoach was needed more now than ever.

You'll notice that, with both examples, I'm straight into it on the calls, I will go on to set out an agenda, as that is important for every single call. But in these situations, before an agenda I want to set the tone, I want to let them know that I'm surprised to hear from them, that I'm not a 'giddy' salesperson excited to get to speak with them again. I do want answers. After all, my job is to get to the truth.

***

I feel a footnote to this 'Returning Prospect' section is needed here:

Don't take it personally when a prospect ghosts you - they don't owe you anything. It's frustrating, sure, but it's part of the game. The key is not to dwell on it, but to learn from it.

If ghosting happens *once in a while*, it's just how sales works. But if it keeps happening, take a hard look at your approach.

- Do you get "happy ears" - hearing what you **want** to hear instead of what's actually being said in a way that leads to you being a hopeful salesperson?
- Are you failing to challenge them in a firm but fair way?
- Are you staying at surface level with respect to understanding and pain points, instead of qualifying the opportunity properly?
- Are you too submissive? Perhaps you bow to every prospect's demand without understanding the *why* behind it? One sign of this is writing and sending proposals far too early.

If ghosting is a recurring theme, the problems probably you. Elite sales professionals are rarely ghosted. They control the process, they set clear expectations and, whether it's a "yes", a "no", or even a "not now", they make it easy for prospects to feel like they can be honest.

So if you're regularly getting ghosted, don't blame the buyer. Fix your game. The agenda in the previous chapter is a great starting point.

Now what?

Once the golden minute is finished, it's over to you.

Here's the common mistakes I see salespeople make at this stage

- They made it obvious they were waiting to speak.
- They pitch slap.
- They talk about the least important thing.

Let me go into each of these in a little more detail.

Making it obvious you were waiting to speak

This can happen throughout the golden minute, not just at the end. Waiting to speak is apparent when the salesperson interrupts and talks over your prospect. If you constantly find yourself doing either of those things, please stop. Both of these things can cause a prospect to become frustrated and shut down. At the end of the golden minute, I can spot a rep who's not been fully listening and just waiting for their chance to speak because they say things like

"Okay, great so what I was looking forward to talking to you about was..."

"Nice, so let me ask some questions"

"Understood, now let me share something with you"

Pitch slap

This is a pretty obvious one, yet I see it a lot. Normally this is because the prospect has thrown so much at the salesperson, they don't know what to do with it. They're almost' "stunned" due to the volume of information given to them - so what do they do? They go into pitch mode. This effectively wastes the golden minute and makes the prospect feel like they've not been heard.

They talk about the least important thing

This is something I see a lot but very few people notice it.

When a prospect shares a load of pain in the golden minute, they typically start with the problem that's top of mind, the thing that is bothering them the most.

Once they start talking they can keep talking and add layers of information on top; they can even go on a tangent. The more they share, the more they remember and it leads to further information being given.

What I tend to see happen at the end of this "download" of information is the salesperson will then latch on to the last thing they heard and start talking about that with the prospect. Think about that for a second; they start to talk about the last thing shared, which is likely to be the least important thing. When you only have a 30-minute call, spending even 5 minutes on the least important thing is crazy.

This happens in life as well; you'll start to notice it. You'll hear people share a load of information, then the person they're sharing it with will ask a question about the very last thing they said. The golden stuff at the start is forgotten and wasted.

Make the prospect feel heard.

Instead of making those mistakes, here's what you're going to do - you're going to make the prospect feel heard, as if you've understood them.

Making a prospect feel heard and understood is one of the most important things you can do early in your discovery calls. Feeling heard builds trust. It makes prospects feel like they can be more open. It makes them feel like they're not just talking to another salesperson who's just ticking their discovery questions off, but instead to someone who actually gets it and cares.

How do you show them you get it, and that you've listened?

Summarise what they just said.

Say something like this:

"Thanks for sharing that; a lot of helpful information there. I've been taking some notes. Do you mind me just taking a minute to play back what I heard?"

Note: In my 10+ years of running discovery calls, nobody has ever said no to this.

A summary is a succinct replay of what they've just said in the golden minute, but there's key things you need to say to make them feel like they've been truly heard by you.

You do that by using their language back at them.

During the golden minute, you must be taking notes; while doing so, it's imperative that you write down the exact language they use, the descriptive and emotional words/phrases they use when articulating their world and problems to you.

Then, when you are summarising, use the exact same language and emphasis back to the prospect. This not only makes them feel heard, but it makes them feel like they're talking to someone who speaks their language - quite literally.

Here are some recent examples of "interesting" words and phrases said to me:

- *"I've promoted two SDRs into AEs and now I'm thinking, "Shit, I don't have the time to give these junior sellers what they need."*
- *"My team are good people, A-players, but unfortunately this isn't an A grade company."*
- *"Some of my reps live in their own echo chamber."*
- *"The sales team I've inherited have never had any formal sales training and I believe that's fundamentally wrong."*
- *"The data shows that, when we get in front of prospects, we win 'frighteningly fast'; unfortunately we're not able to get in front of enough prospects."*
- *"I'm spinning a lot of plates and I'm about to drop some; and when I do its going to create one hell of a mess."*

When I've summarised back I've used the exact phrases back to them.

Once I've finished summarising, I say the same thing

"I think that's everything you shared, would you say that's a fair summary?

As mentioned earlier, the word "fair" is great in situations like this, for a number of reasons:

1. It signals that you're being objective and not running the call with your own agenda.

2. It gives the prospect a sense of control - people like to feel like their perspective has been both heard and understood accurately. By asking if your summary is fair, you're handing them the authority to confirm or correct it.

3. On the flip side, later in the call they can't go back on any of the points, if they were to do so they'd be going back on their own words. People can't argue with their own words. This is also another reason why it's so important to listen intently to what they say in the golden minute (and throughout all of your conversations), and re-use their exact words in your summary.

4. It softens potential disagreement - if they think you've missed the mark (which from time to time, will happen), framing it by asking "is that fair" makes them more likely to gently correct you than to push back aggressively.

If you've summarised the golden minute well, you'll often get praise/positive feedback like so:

"Wow, you really were listening"; "On the money"; "You said it better than I did".

Quick tip: to take effective notes you need to get good at touch typing. It takes practice, but you want to be able to type while looking at your prospect. Having good notes along with call transcripts and summaries also really helps when using AI to summarise. Load all of them into ChatGPT for example, and you'll get a much better, quicker summary/notes and action items.

Now just because the prospect has said 'well done' for the summary, doesn't mean you move on. You ask one further question
Ask them this:

"Is there anything else you think I need to know?"

I'd say this is a 60/40 split in terms of what happens next. About 60% of the time they'll say "No, or "You've got it all", but 40% of the time they'll pause to think and then tell you something else that will help you. Examples include: additional insight on budgets, stakeholders, other problems they have.

While it only works 40% of the time, I ask it every time.

Summary

The *Golden Minute* is crucial. This is the moment your prospect starts talking, often unfiltered; your job is to make sure it's uninterrupted - let them talk freely about their challenges while you pay close attention to their specifically chosen words, tone and emphasis. When you think they've finished speaking, keep quiet; they will often reload and fill the silence with more information.

Once they have stopped speaking, your summary and first question are crucial.

Coupled with a strong agenda, this part of the call sets the tone for the entire conversation - if you miss it, you're playing catch-up the rest of the way.

Chapter Six

Getting to Compelling Reasons to Buy

I have had the benefit of speaking with hundreds of sales leaders over the past decade. These have ranged from small startups through to those running teams in large FTSE 100 companies.

When I ask them what one thing they see their best salespeople doing differently in discovery calls, the number one answer I hear is "Rich - quite simply they ask better questions."

And while I understand what they mean by this, my interpretation of what they are *really* saying is, "They do a better job of understanding our buyers."

Until we learn about our prospect's situation, their challenges, and desires, a deal will never ever go anywhere.

To learn stuff, we have to ask questions.

But here's the key thing. It's not just asking "better questions" that gives better outcomes in discovery calls. It's asking the right question at the right time; It's asking questions which don't feel self-serving and instead, that feel like questions designed to help the prospect; It's *how* you ask certain questions; this can be the difference between being perceived as a salesperson rather than a truly trusted advisor.

But ultimately, what is the point of asking better questions at the right time?

It is all about unlocking the prospect's compelling reasons to move away from their current state, and move towards a state where they make a decision to work with you.

Having listened to quite literally thousands of recorded discovery calls over my career, I've seen how a salesperson's effectiveness at getting to compelling reasons to buy has been the difference between prospects shrugging their shoulders at the end of the call to them asking the salesperson how quickly they can get the next call scheduled in.

Last year, Objective Management Group (the world leader in sales team evaluations) assessed around 75,000 salespeople. Their assessment shows that 38% of all salespeople are "Weak" at consultative selling, with 40% "Serviceable". Alarmingly, that shows that nearly 80% of salespeople do not have an effective strategy for asking questions, and thus understanding a prospect's compelling reason/s to buy.

So why do so many struggle with it?

For me, it boils down to five things:

- They don't have a clear understanding of what they need to have learned by the end of a discovery call, in order to move an opportunity forward.

- They have been overly confused by complex methodologies which (ironically) have been designed to help the salesperson.

- They *think* that what they are hearing from a prospect are strong buying signals or pain points when, in reality, all they are hearing are surface level issues.

- They are scared or nervous of asking prospects challenging or tough questions. They think it will offend them or derail a deal. (This is called having a high need for approval).

- They are poor at active listening. This means they don't ask questions based on what they are hearing. Instead, they ask the questions they are pre-programmed to ask. (as they are written down on a notepad or discovery call playbook somewhere).

When looking at the above, it's easy to see why so many people struggle. There appear to be so many moving parts needing to be considered by a seller conducting discovery. That's before you add in the complexities of humans and differing personalities.

And ultimately there's a reason as to why those who have a top class question strategy are the ones who are making the most commission.

The Four Killer Questions

Over the years, and from the many deals I have won, and the even larger number that I have lost, I realised that my question strategy needed to be built around getting answers to the following four killer questions. I've studied and learned a number of different methodologies and qualification frameworks over the years, but when I peeled it all back, if I didn't have good answers to the questions below, I knew it was a deal I wasn't able to forecast accurately.

Killer Question One: Does this prospect have a problem I can solve?

Seems simplistic. But I think back to my early days of selling and I simply wasted too much time trying to push a square peg product into a round-hole problem.

I remember once speaking with a prospect who was looking to buy a basic cloud call recording platform. I instead pushed our conversation intelligence platform at him. It was like trying to sell a Ferrari to someone looking for a Ford Focus. In hindsight (and after investing a ton of time into follow-up activities), the prospect finally told me that he had bought a basic cloud phone system.

This is a tough lesson, but it is still being learned by many salespeople.

A good way of divulging whether a prospect has a problem you can solve, is by listening to the words that come out of their mouth when they describe their problems. Are these the words that you have heard from others who went on to buy from you? If you listen back to the calls for the deals your team are marking as "closed won", you should quickly see there are some commonalities there.

Killer Question Two: How big is the problem?

Many salespeople hear the prospect talk about a problem that they know they can solve and quickly get happy ears. *They've just told me that they are a bit frustrated with their internal expense management process...that's exactly how we help. Woohoo!*

Here's the thing. We all live with things that irritate and frustrate us. Many things. But the things which get our attention and action, are the things which arise as BIG problems.

For example, I have a four-slice toaster. For some reason, only half of the toaster is working. It's annoying. It bugs me. But it's not a BIG problem. It just means that, at any time in my household, we can only be toasting two slices of bread. In other words, I can live with it.

Remember what I was saying earlier. If the problem you are solving is not in the top three things on the prospect's priority list to solve, then it's probably something they can live with.

It's your job to understand not just whether the prospect is suffering a problem you know you can solve. But you also need to understand how big a problem it is.

Killer Question Three: Does the prospect want to start solving the problem NOW (or at least in the very near future)?

Most BIG problems will definitely be getting solved right away, won't they?

Well... in theory that makes sense.

But human behaviour shows us that, even big problems that weigh on our mind, are sometimes problems we aren't motivated to take action on.

I knew one year out from my wedding day that I really needed to lose at least a stone of weight so that I could look and feel better on what would be one of the best days of my life. It was something that weighed on my mind every day. But the reality? I kicked the can down the road for a number of months.

Thankfully, I lost weight. But the reality is, when a big problem came along, I didn't take action when I really should have. Motivation. Time. Focus. Fear of failure. Anxiety of making a wrong decision. All of these things were reasons why I didn't ultimately invest resources into addressing the problem.

I remember once selling to a prospect, who told me they were at potential risk of losing out on possible revenue of £2.5m as a result of a poor and slow onboarding process for the new hire drive they were about to embark on. It was a big problem, but they didn't buy a solution to that problem from me. The reason? The bigger problem they were focused on solving was getting better results from their *existing* team. This made it an £8m problem.

Understanding why a prospect cares about solving their big problem *now* will enable you to:

- Know compelling dates by which your prospect will need to implement your product/service.

- Allow you to re-enforce the cost of inaction through the buying process.
- Learn who else in the business is motivated to solve the problem.
- Invest more time and resources in the deal.

Consider this in your discovery process. Don't just be satisfied when you have identified a problem and even quantified it as a big problem. You need to get the prospect confirming to you that they want to take action now.

Killer Question Four: Why you rather than the competition?

OK, so the prospect has confirmed that they want to solve their big business problem quickly. The final question that needs answering is why should they opt to choose you to fix it rather than somebody else. What's key here is remembering that other options may include trying to tackle it internally and not using you **or** your competition.

It's amazing how many sellers get the answers to the previous questions, but then fail to give their buyer the answer to this one. They simply assume that, because they have found themselves with someone with a big problem they can solve, and they are motivated to solve it now, the prospect isn't thinking about other options.

Let me tell you that most buyers today will be looking at other options. Particularly in today's economy, where they are being told by CEOs and CFOs to go overboard on due diligence. Particularly at a time when there is seemingly more competition than ever before in such crowded markets.

I remember painfully losing a deal which was into its third month of the sales cycle. I was convinced that, given all the communication and progress we had made in the deal over a "top priority" issue, that I was destined to win the deal. After forecasting it as a "Most Likely" deal several times in my pipeline updates, I was shocked one morning to hear that they had chosen another vendor. I felt blindsided, but the truth is - I had simply assumed that we were the only horse in the race. I hadn't once even asked the prospect if they were considering other options.

Do not assume that you are in pole position. Do not think that by not bringing up the competition that you are increasing the chances of the buyer not looking at them.

It is your job in discovery to establish *why* people buy from you versus others. And not only that, but you need to understand situations where people buy from your competition. By the way, let's not forget that our BIGGEST competitor is the status quo. The competitor called "let's do nothing".

In discovery, make sure that you are helping the buyer understand your differentiated approach to solving the problem they are describing to you. And the specific capabilities that make you the best choice, for the situation they are in.

The worst thing you can do is have your prospect leave a call feeling like they have little idea as to "why you rather than the next company they are scheduled to speak with later that day".

Getting to Pain - The Inverted Pyramid of Pain

So now we understand WHAT we want to uncover in our discovery calls, the key question is HOW you reveal those answers.

What are the specific questions and approaches that enable us to go from understanding the problems our prospects are facing (and that we can solve), through to quantifying how much they really care about solving them.

This for me, is the biggest difference I see in top performing salespeople to those who struggle.

It is the ability to identify compelling reasons why someone would move away from their current state, to one where they are committed to changing.

Our choice of questions, how we ask those questions, and when we ask those questions is crucial here. Get one of those elements wrong, and you run the risk of losing all credibility and trust with your prospects.

In the following section, I'm going to bring to life how you would go about using specific lines of questioning to go from surface level pain with a prospect, all the way down to their personal compelling reasons for buying from you. I call this the inverted pyramid of pain.

The diagram is broken down into five levels including Surface Level Pain. What is interesting is that I find that each horizontal line of the pyramid reflects the number of salespeople who are well equipped to effectively reach each level. The most significant number of salespeople are well equipped to identify surface level pain or issues from their prospects. The problem is, these are never the key reasons why somebody will buy. The fewest number of salespeople are able to consistently reach Level 3 or Level 4 in the pyramid. This is where prospects will reveal their true motivations for buying, and share the impact of staying in their current state on both their business and also themselves as individuals.

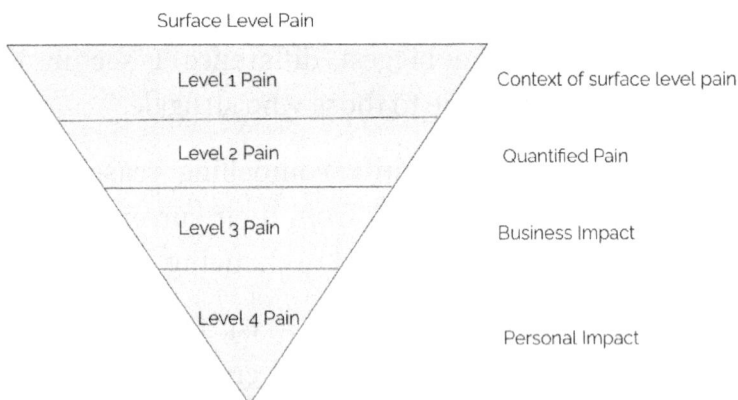

Surface Level Pain

Level 1 Pain	Context of surface level pain
Level 2 Pain	Quantified Pain
Level 3 Pain	Business Impact
Level 4 Pain	Personal Impact

In the following pages, I am going to give more context as to what each of these levels looks and sounds like in a discovery conversation, along with specific types of questions you can leverage to enable you to move your prospect down the pyramid.

Surface Level Pain

Here is what I have identified from listening to thousands of discovery calls over the past decade.

Most prospects will fairly easily share surface level reasons as to why they have an interest in your product or service.

What does surface level pain sound like?

Below is a list of key words and phrases that I have identified are common signals of surface level pain:

- Need to improve performance.
- Want to be more efficient.
- Interested in help with coaching.
- Looking for a way to automate this process.
- Would like to increase confidence.
- We do it quite manually right now.
- Looking for some sales training.
- Need some visibility into security.

All of these phrases indicate an underlying issue, but ultimately look, feel, and sound like "nice to solve" problems. A good way of identifying whether you are hearing surface level pain from your prospect, is if they are using "solution-based language". In other words, they are looking for the solution to a problem as opposed to talking about the real problem at hand. "Looking for some sales training" is solution-based language. The prospect is seeking the solution as opposed to sharing what exactly they want sales training to fix.

Below are two transcripts of a discovery which showcases a conversation between a seller and a buyer. In the first example, the seller is getting stuck at surface level pain and rushes their discovery. In the second example, the seller goes beyond surface level pain using effective questioning and works their way down the inverted pyramid of pain.

Example One

Salesperson: *"What was it that piqued your interest in speaking with me today?"*

Prospect: *"So we've been reviewing our objectives for the year ahead as a sales team, and I was intrigued to learn more about the type of sales coaching support you may be able to give our reps."*

Salesperson: *"Great! And what is it about sales coaching specifically that you're interested in?"*

Prospect: *"Our sales managers are low on bandwidth, so I'm curious about how we could give our team some help to lift performance."*

Salesperson: *"No worries. Let me share how we help others with that..."*

Notice that the prospect here is using solution-based language out of the gate, which indicates the surface level pain. In this case, "sales coaching" is a solution. It's not the problem. Secondly, the salesperson *thinks* they have heard true business pain, when in fact all they have heard is that the "sales managers are low on bandwidth". This is at best, Level 1 pain on the pyramid. There's an argument to say that it is no more than another flavour of surface level pain. Finally, the salesperson has ignored the killer phrase used by the prospect "help to lift performance".

Instead, they have rushed straight into pitch mode. If the seller had explored this further, they could have found a path to working their way down the pyramid and getting to the crux of the real issue at hand.

From experience, 90% of discovery calls I listen to look and sound like this call. Sellers rarely get beyond surface level issues and, as such, they rarely ever get to truly understanding their prospect's situation. When they don't understand their buyers, then no wonder they struggle to sell.

Example 2

Let's look at the same starting point, but this time the salesperson successfully gets to Level 4 pain on the pyramid. We will break down the questions they are using afterwards.

Salesperson: *"What was it that piqued your interest in speaking with me today?"*

This is a great question to create demand in your discovery calls. If a prospect has committed valuable time to agreeing to meet with you, then it's unlikely they will just be there for the good of their health. Asking this question encourages them to share a genuine reason why they wanted to meet with you. Moreover, "piqued interest" is designed to be very low commitment. You're not asking them to share their deepest, darkest problems straight out the gate. You're simply asking them what made them even slightly motivated to meet with you. More times than not, what you will hear next is surface level pain. That is a great starting point.

Prospect: *"So we've been reviewing our objectives for the year ahead as a sales team, and I was intrigued to learn more about the type of sales coaching support you may be able to give our reps." (Surface level)*

Salesperson: *"Great! You mentioned your objectives for the year ahead. Can you tell me more about that?*

Most salespeople here will move straight towards focusing on the "sales coaching support" element of what the prospect has just shared. Why? Because they feel like it's an open invitation to start talking about the solution they can provide. The key here is to not rush to solutions. The key is to explore the reason why the prospect is looking for a solution. When a prospect mentions things like "objectives", "challenges" or 'focuses', then these indicate strategic topics that have business priority attached to them.

There are two key aspects to the prospect's response I want to examine here. Firstly, note the repetition of the prospect's words back at them. This is a great tactic to show the prospect you are listening, but also focusing the conversation on things the prospect has chosen to share. Secondly, one of my favourite questions to ask in discovery is, "Can you tell me more about that?" Salespeople agonise over creating smart, intelligent, wordsmithed questions. But the best questions are those that simply get the prospect to share more. The more they share, the more you learn. The more you learn, the better positioned you are to identify areas you may be able to help.

Prospect: *"We need to grow sales by 40% this year. We're not expecting a meaningful increase in marketing leads and we've identified that one of the main levers for us to pull is improving our conversion rates." (Level 1)*

Salesperson: *"OK. And when you say 'improving conversion rates', would you be able to share more about what your conversion rates are today?"*

This question is designed to help move the prospect from Level 1 to a Level 2 state, where they begin to quantify the problem they have. This not only helps to profile how clear the prospect is on the size of the problem, but also enables you to paint a picture in your own head as to how much you can realistically help them address the problem. Whenever a prospect tells you that they are trying to improve a metric, don't rush prematurely to pitching a solution. Use it as an opportunity to understand what that metric looks like today, and why they aren't happy with it. You're probably noticing a trend here. Don't rush to pitch. Spend time exploring the problem. This is what makes the best salespeople stand out from the rest in discovery.

Prospect: *"We tend to convert 20% of qualified opportunities to 'closed won', though it does vary across the team" (Level 2)*

Salesperson: *"I appreciate you sharing that. What have you observed about why deals don't convert?"*

Here I am looking for the prospect to give me some specific context as to why they are not making the progress they wish they were. My choice of the words "what have you observed here" are carefully chosen. Before I provide any type of personal expertise or opinion, I want the prospect to tell me what they have seen and heard with their own eyes and ears. It is far more powerful for your prospect to tell you why they think they have the problem, and for you to validate it, as opposed to you just telling the prospect what you think.

Prospect: *"When I listen to calls, I observe that we don't do a very good job at identifying compelling reasons for prospects to buy. Our discovery needs a lot of work. We didn't have to work as hard at it when we were getting loads of inbound leads, but that's all changed now."*

Salesperson: *"Interesting. I've heard the same from a few VPs of Sales this year. They similarly talk about their lack of inbound leads and the importance of needing to make more from outbound generated leads. When you say... 'needs a lot of work', what have you tried so far to address it?"*

I start here by sharing my expertise and the social proof I have accumulated from speaking with like-minded prospects. This is a good strategy to make the prospect feel like they aren't the only one, but also that they are probably talking to the right person, who is well informed on the specific issue they are sharing with you. Following this, now that I've got a sense of the problem and the size of it, I want to try and rule out the possibility that the prospect could think that trying to address this internally is still a good option for them. Remember, the status quo is always going to be a desirable option for any business if it means making use of existing resources rather than investing in external ones. Asking the prospect if they have already tried to fix the problem is a good way of divulging this. Not only this, but it also shows further evidence that this is a problem they actually care about.

Prospect: *"Well I try and do a lot of coaching on calls and deals, but ultimately my bandwidth is massively stretched. I just don't have the time to do it consistently enough with a team of eight reps"*

Salesperson: *"Do you mind if I ask a bit of a direct question? Do you believe you can achieve your revenue goals this year if you don't address this problem in the near term?*

This is where I am getting to both business and personal pain. In this case, both the company and the prospect's goals are at risk if they don't fix their sales conversion issue. Moreover, I've asked them if they believe these problems need to be fixed in the "near term". Here is where I am getting an answer to Killer Question Number Three. Is this a problem that the prospect needs to fix quickly? I'll admit I used to feel it was my job as a salesperson to artificially create urgency. I no longer believe this. I don't believe you can "create urgency" with your prospects. Instead, you have to identify if there is a sense of urgency so you can align with it. Remember, people buy for their own reasons - not yours.

Notice my prelude to asking the question. I asked the prospect if they were OK with me asking a direct question. This is a great tactic when you are going to be asking prospects tough or somewhat uncomfortable questions. Not only do you get their permission (they will almost ALWAYS give you permission), but they psychologically brace themselves for the tough question. As a result, they are more likely to give a direct and honest answer back. Note that you can't just ask these questions straight out of the gate. You have to earn the right to ask them. And that comes with asking the right lead-up questions, which demonstrate a solid understanding of their situation.

Prospect: *"I don't believe so... no." (Level 3)*

Salesperson: *"Imagine if we were sitting talking in 12 months; what would success look like for you personally if we made progress here?"*

After getting to pain, I always find it helpful to move the prospect to thinking about a positive future. This not only makes them feel like you aren't just there to make them feel bad about their situation, but that you're also there to help them find success. Framing the questions as "what would success look like for you personally?" is my way of getting the prospect to share the personal win they will get if they address the problem being discussed. Tying a personal win to the problem gets the prospect away from just thinking about business success, to what they themselves could benefit from. This creates a much more powerful sentiment. Also note my use of the words "if we made progress". This is intentional, as I want the prospect to start thinking about us winning together - as a partnership.

Prospect: *"If we got the team to that 40% conversion level, it would be huge. I'd be in a much stronger position to unlock a CRO role in the business." (Level 4)*

And there you have it. This is how you can use questions to get you down the pyramid of pain in your discovery calls. Hopefully, you will see that there isn't anything hugely complicated in the conversation above. These aren't 50 questions you need to write down on a piece of paper to ask your prospect before your call. They aren't intelligently crafted and overly thought out to "gotcha" your prospect. They are questions designed to get your prospect to share more information, and to feel comfortable opening up, and ultimately to reveal the reality of their situation. If you count back, I only asked seven questions to go from surface level pain to understanding the business and personal impact of the problem.

That's not me saying it's easy. Feeling confident asking these questions in a conversational and curious fashion takes practice and intentional listening. My point here is that sales doesn't need to be complicated.

Why you rather than the competition?

At some point in the discovery conversation, you must help the prospect understand *why you are best positioned to solve their problem* - not just why you are "better" than competitors.

So what are some of the biggest mistakes people make here when it comes to answering the question from prospects about "why you?"

1. Being Too Generic. Statements like *"We specialise in efficiency"* are vague and could apply to countless competitors.

- If your positioning sounds like any one of multiple companies, it is not strong enough.

2. Focusing Too Much on Features

- Saying *"We have AI-powered automation"* does not explain why that matters or when it is the right choice for the buyer.

- Features do not position your product - it is the value they create that does.

3. Ignoring Competitive Alternatives

- Buyers always compare you to something else - whether it is a competitor or sticking with the status quo.

- If you do not proactively address these alternatives, the buyer will fill in the gaps themselves. Often that can result in them making an incorrect assumption.

4. Failing to Clarify Who Shouldn't Buy

- Strong positioning acknowledges when another option might be a better fit. This is often the path that a lot of salespeople veer away from, as they believe that every prospect is right for them. Actually, when you acknowledge those companies you are not a good fit for, it can become a selling superpower.

- Saying *"If X is particularly important for you, then we are probably not the right solution. However if Y is really important to you, then that's one of the main reasons people choose to work with us"* builds credibility and ensures you win the right customers - which is not every customer.

How to Deliver a Strong Positioning Statement

So what do you do when a prospect asks, "Can you tell me about your company then?"

- Instead of jumping into a list of features and benefits, craft a positioning statement that:
  - Connects the dots between your discovery questions and their pain points.
  - Explains why you are uniquely positioned to solve their problem.

- Remember, you can only do this effectively if you have understood their compelling reasons to buy!!

- Resist the product pitch. Do not talk about why you are better than competitors - talk about why you are uniquely suited to solving the prospect's problem.

Below is a handy framework to help you craft your positioning statement:

1. Replay the Prospect's Problems.

Restate their key pain points to show understanding and alignment.

2. Competitive Alternatives.

Identify what the prospect would do if your solution didn't exist (competitors, internal solutions, or doing nothing).

3. Situations Where the Competitive Alternative Might Be the Better Option.

Acknowledge scenarios where a competitor or alternative approach might be a better fit.

4. Why You Are Likely the Better Option Based on the Prospect's Situation.

Explain how your unique approach is the best choice for their specific needs.

5. Your Differentiated Capabilities.

Highlight what makes your product or solution unique and why that difference matters to the prospect.

As a working example, let's imagine I am providing a positioning statement for MySalesCoach. Here's what it would sound like:

1. "So from our conversation, you mentioned that one of the big problems you have is you have a team of AEs who each need support, but they are all at different levels of ability and tenure."
2. "One of the options it sounds like you've already tried is to find the time to coach internally, or to perhaps consider external training companies."

3. "If you had told me that you were looking for some one-size-fits-all sales training for the team, I would probably suggest we may not be the best option."
4. "But given the fact you feel the team all have unique needs, then that's where people typically choose to work with us."
5. "That's because of our heavy focus on 1:1 coaching, where we match each rep to their perfect coach."

Your goal isn't to tell your prospect why you are "better". It's to be different in a way that actually matters to your ideal customer.

Chapter Seven

The Power of Storytelling in Sales

Why Storytelling is a Sales Superpower

My oldest son, William (6), must have 50+ books in his bedroom, ranging from Julia Donaldson's picture books to the classics by Roald Dahl. While he'd tell you he loved them all, if you asked him to pick out his favourites he'd pick out the following;

- William You're Amazing.
- William Solves a Mystery.
- William Helps the Gingerbread Boy.
- William's Really Wild School.
- Charlie's Big Brother, William.

Notice something? He's the star of his favourite stories. The books where you get the child's name printed in the book are always popular. These are the books he asks for most nights.

Why? Because people love stories where they can picture themselves in the narrative. They don't want to hear about someone else's success - they want to see how they fit into it.

And that's why storytelling is a game-changer in sales. It's not just about making your product sound good; it's about making your *prospect* the star of the story. It's about helping them imagine a better version of themselves, a version where they're more successful and more efficient - they are hitting their goals, and making themselves look good to their boss.

Stories also last in the memory- research suggests that, when we hear information in the form of a story, we retain around 65-70% of it - compared to just 5-10% when something is delivered as raw statistics. That can't be ignored; it's why the best reps don't just present. They tell stories that make prospects feel the pain, see the opportunity in front of them and, ultimately, take action.

The Three Sales Stories Every AE Needs

Through our experience and coaching AEs, we've identified three types of stories that, when they are used correctly, can be incredibly powerful in discovery calls. Each serves a different purpose and should be used at the right moment to help the prospect see themselves as the hero of their journey.

1. The Vision Story - What Does Success Look Like?

Sometimes, your prospect hasn't yet imagined what "better" looks like. Your job is to paint that picture for them and help them step into that future.

When to Use It:

- Early in the conversation to spark curiosity.
- When the prospect seems stuck in the status quo.
- To shift focus from product features to business impact.
- When they're pushing you for ROI

Example of a Story I Tell

Let's say a prospect asks me about expected ROI:

"Let's look at how you'll measure ROI yourself, let's imagine it's 12 months from now. You're sitting down with your CEO to discuss the renewal with MySalesCoach, what's changed in your world to make this renewal a no-brainer?"

This approach gets them to describe their own future success, which is far more compelling than you trying to sell it to them. It also gives me a window of what ROI really means to them and how they'll measure the impact of our services. An average rep would just start talking about ROI but people measure ROI differently, so tap into how they view it by getting them to paint a picture of what success looks like further down the line, as a result of working with you.

Why this works:

- It makes them emotionally invested in change.
- It forces them to think beyond "features" and consider long-term impact.
- It subtly positions your solution as the bridge between where they are now and where they want to be.

- They only ever paint the best possible picture; now this is what you can focus the conversations on, helping them turn that vision into reality.

2. The Social Proof Story - Why Do Others Choose Us?

This is all about reducing risk for the prospect. Buyers don't like feeling like they're taking a gamble. If you can show them that others in their situation have already successfully made the change, it lowers their fear of making the wrong decision.

When to use it:

- When a prospect is skeptical about change.
- To validate a key challenge or concern.
- To provide proof that your solution works in real-world scenarios.

Example:

"What you just said reminds me of a conversation I had with another VP of Sales last week. They told me their team was struggling to move beyond surface level discovery, and as a result, their deals kept stalling. They started using MySalesCoach to provide targeted coaching, and, within six months, their win rates had jumped by 18%. Should we spend the rest of our time talking about how a similar programme could help you and your team achieve similar results?"

Why this works:

- It subtly reinforces that your solution is trusted by others.

- It keeps the focus on their pain rather than jumping straight to a pitch.
- It encourages them to open up further about their situation.
- It gets them imagining a scenario where they're more successful than they are today.

3. The Personal Experience Story - Why Do I Care About This Problem

We accept for many this is the hardest story to tell - yet it is the most powerful. It's hard, because to deliver it with credibility you really need to have sat in their seat, and experienced this pain first hand. If you have, you can tell a relevant story that builds credibility and trust.

When to use it:

- When you have a direct, relatable experience.
- To establish credibility and relatability.
- When the prospect needs reassurance that you understand their world.

Example:

"I completely understand what you're going through. When I was a VP of Sales, I too felt like I was constantly firefighting. One minute I was in back-to-back deal reviews, the next I was being pulled into an exec meeting, and all the while, I had this nagging feeling that I wasn't giving my team the coaching they needed. That frustration - the knowledge that I was stuck on a hamster wheel, what you just said reminded me of that exact feeling".

Why this works:

- It makes you credible and relatable.
- It builds trust quickly.
- It naturally creates a space for you to ask deeper, tougher discovery questions

Caution: Use this sparingly. If you overdo personal stories, you risk making the call about you rather than the prospect. Timing is everything.

What if you haven't experienced the problem first-hand?

Even if you haven't personally sat in their seat and faced the same challenges as your prospect, you may still have a powerful way to connect - your own experience as a **user** of the product you're selling. Let me explain, if you're selling a solution that you actively use, you can explain how it has impacted your own workflow. This makes the conversation more natural and allows the prospect to see how their own team could benefit in the same way.

For example:

"I totally get why you're asking about adoption - it's something we think about a lot too. I actually use our own platform every day. The structured insights and automation save me hours each week and help me focus on the right deals. If your team had access to the same level of efficiency and visibility, how do you think that would impact their performance?"

By framing it this way, you make their team the focus of the story while subtly demonstrating the product's value through your own usage.

When you are a product of your own product

Some of you are living proof of what you sell - you use your own product every day, and that is naturally reflected in the way you work. For example:

- **If you sell a conversational intelligence tool**, you probably ask better questions and handle objections smoothly.
- **If you sell an AI-powered writing assistant**, your emails and messaging will be polished and effective.
- **If you sell a sales enablement tool**, your ability to pull up relevant insights and collateral on demand will be unmatched.

When you're a product of what you sell, prospects will notice. This often leads to compliments like:

- *"I wish my team followed up like that."*
- *"You're really structured in how you run these calls - I wish my reps worked like that."*
- *"Your messaging is so clear - how do you do it?"*

These moments are golden opportunities - don't just brush them off.

Instead of simply saying "Thanks," turn the compliment into a bridge to your product's value.

A strong response could be:

"I really appreciate that! To be honest, it's because I use our own platform every day - it helps me stay structured and consistent without having to think about it. That's exactly why so many teams invest in this - because it makes these behaviors repeatable for everyone, not just the top performers"

After you've said that, then go quiet. They'll be creating a story in their head of what would happen if their team were just like you.

This approach does three things:

1. **It reinforces credibility** - you're not just selling the product; you're a success story that proves its value.
2. **It shifts the focus back to them** - you've shown what's possible, and now they're thinking about their own team.
3. **It creates a natural transition into a deeper conversation** - rather than just accepting the compliment, which can be awkward, (particularly for us Brits) you use it to explore their needs further.

Being a walking proof of your product's impact is one of the most powerful (and under-utilised) sales tools. Use it to your advantage.

The Biggest Storytelling Mistakes AEs Make

- Talking too much about yourself. Your stories should reinforce their situation, not turn into a monologue about you.

- Telling stories with no clear takeaway. Every story should drive the conversation forward.
- Making it too long. Keep stories to 30-60 seconds max.
- Ignoring emotional language. The best stories tap into frustration, hope, and aspiration.

Build Your Own Story Bank

You don't need 100 stories - you just need a handful of well-crafted, repeatable ones. Here's how to build your personal story bank:

1. Identify real customer wins and challenges. Work with your customer success team to gather insights.
2. Write them out and learn them but also have them saved for quick access.
3. Practice delivering them naturally. Storytelling is a skill - you get better with repetition.
4. Use them in your next call. The more you use them, the sharper they become.

Final Thought: The Best Sales Stories Are the Ones Where They're the Hero

The best sales stories aren't about your product - they're about your prospect. They're the stories that make them see themselves in a better future, where they're more successful, their job is easier, and they're getting the recognition they deserve. Facts and features are forgettable, but a great story sticks because it makes them *feel* the impact of change before they even make a decision.

Master storytelling, and you won't just explain why they should change - you'll make them *want* to. You'll create a vision they can step into, remove the fear of risk by showing them others who have succeeded, and build credibility by proving you understand their world.

At the end of the day, the most powerful sales conversation isn't one where you convince them - it's one where they convince themselves.

Chapter Eight

Objections

"Objection" - this is the one word that can make a sales professional tense up and squirm.

Like a pothole appearing out of nowhere on the smoothest road, an objection can hit at any moment in the sales cycle - even in deals you're confident you will close. And because of that, objections often trigger a knee-jerk reaction. Your mind scrambles for a response, fearing that saying the wrong thing will scupper the deal. Your gut reaction is usually one of two things: go ultra-defensive and insist they're wrong, or go ultra-aggressive in an attempt to win them over.

Sticking with the analogy, if you're "experienced" and you've been driving the same road for a while then, on a clear day, you'll probably see the pothole coming. It's the same on a sales call - you know what objection the prospect is about to give, you're already prepared with your talk track, your "go to" response. When you nail an objection it feels good, right? They've thrown you a potential bomb, and you've disarmed it instantly.

Sound familiar?

And that's part of the problem, we see objections as nasty potholes, here to ruin our deals.

We see them as things to fear, avoid, overcome and beat.

What if we saw objections differently?

Instead of deal breakers, what if we viewed objections as a window into the buyer's mind - an opportunity to understand what they're thinking, what they fear and what truly matters to them. Dealing with objections isn't about having the perfect comeback, it's about understanding the reasons behind them and using those reasons to unlock further discovery - the more information you gather, the better you can qualify and position your offering over the competition.

What Even Is an Objection?

An objection is either a signal that your prospect has a concern, a gap in their understanding that needs to be addressed or something they're curious about.

With concerns, you get a clearer insight into how they think i.e., risk perception, decision-making style or priorities. Concerns are often shaped by past experiences, giving insight into where they've tried and failed to solve their problem before, for instance. Understanding their concerns allows you to address them effectively, build trust, and guide them toward a solution that aligns with their needs.

When someone raises an objection due to a gap in their knowledge, it reveals where they need clarity and what assumptions they're making. I often remind my sales team, "A confused mind never buys." When a prospect is unclear or making assumptions, confusion can stall their decision-making. Identifying these gaps allows you to address misconceptions, provide clarity, and guide them toward a more confident, informed decision.

When a prospect raises an objection out of curiosity, it's a great sign - they're engaged, thinking critically, and probably considering the bigger picture beyond the sale. It signals interest rather than resistance, giving you the chance to educate, build value, and deepen the conversation. When you're seen as a trusted advisor, a curious objection becomes an opportunity to shape their perspective, uncover deeper needs, and position your solution as the best fit - leading to a more meaningful and productive sales discussion.

Sometimes, digging deeper into objections can reveal red flags - signs that a prospect might not be the right fit or isn't fully committed to solving their problem. For example, if they keep fixating on price without considering value, or hesitate despite acknowledging the problem, they may not be serious about moving forward. If you're going to lose, lose fast. Identifying these red flags early helps you focus your time and energy on prospects who are truly ready to take action.

What Isn't an Objection?

When coaching on objection handling, I often find myself saying, "That's not an objection, that's a statement, that's a reaction, that's a question, or that's a negotiation tactic." For example:

A Statement is a neutral or factual remark, not necessarily signalling resistance such as *"we already* *work with a competitor,"* which can understandably feel like a competitor-based objection. But it's not, it's just a fact, not resistance. Another example might be, "We don't have a budget for this right now." This will feel like a price objection, but it might not be, it could be a financial reality, which doesn't mean they're not interested.

A Reaction is an emotional or knee-jerk response based on first impressions, rather than a well-thought-out objection. Remember, you're a professional seller. You're not always dealing with a professional buyer; they may only buy two or three things a year at best. A classic example of a reaction is "Whoa, that's expensive." This automatically feels like a price objection, but it's not. It's a knee-jerk reaction based on sticker shock. This also may suggest you've gone to pricing too soon.

A Question can sometimes sound and feel like an objection, when really they're just looking for more information. For example they may ask, "Who else do you work with?" To us, this may feel like an objection based on skepticism about the product's credibility, when really they're asking for more information, specifically wanting social proof to help them feel more confident.

A Negotiation Tactic isn't an objection; it's your prospects testing their leverage rather than truly resisting. This is more common with experienced buyers. Recognising negotiation tactics helps you stay in control and respond effectively. A classic one is, "We wouldn't commit to a 12-month contract." This is perhaps closer to an objection, but it can feel like a deal-breaker when really it's a negotiation tactic to gain flexibility or better terms.

In summary, not every hesitation or pushback is a true objection. Understanding the difference between statements, reactions, questions, and negotiation tactics allows you to respond appropriately without getting defensive or derailing the conversation. Instead of treating everything as resistance, take a step back, clarify intent, and guide the discussion toward value; we'll show you how to do that in this chapter. Ultimately, the better you get at recognising these nuances, the more effectively you will be able to move deals forward with confidence and control.

Why Do We Even Get Objections?

Objections happen for a reason, and they tend to come from five main sources... apologies in advance, but you're not going to like the last one...

1. **Uncertainty** - "I don't fully understand this yet."

When a prospect says something like *"I'm not sure how this would fit into what we're already doing"* or *"We've already got something in place for this,"* what they're really saying is *"I don't fully see the need and impact of what you are offering."*

This isn't resistance; it's a knowledge gap. They're still trying to figure out whether this makes sense for them, but instead of admitting, "I don't get it" (because no one likes saying that out loud), they mask it as an objection.

This usually happens because the discovery wasn't deep enough, meaning you didn't fully uncover their current state, pain points, or priorities, so your solution feels disconnected. It can also happen when context is skipped, or when you've gone too quickly into features or benefits, without bridging it back to what they do today.

If they're not clear on how your product works, how it helps, how it compares to their current approach, or why they need it, their default reaction is to say no.

2. Risk Perception - "What if this goes wrong?"

Some objections aren't about understanding; they're about fear. Prospects worry about:

- Making the wrong decision.
- Wasting time and company money.
- Looking bad internally if this fails - this is when you'll hear things like:
    - ☐ *"We tried something like this before, and it didn't work."*
    - ☐ *"I don't think my team will use this."*
    - ☐ *"Can we do a pilot or free trial before committing?"*

People fear risk and loss more than they anticipate reward. If they don't feel like they're making a safe and obvious decision, they'll hesitate, stall, or walk away entirely. This is one main reason more and more stakeholders unnecessarily get involved in deals; your prospect wants to share the risk of a bad decision. When I ask salespeople who their biggest competitor is, they will always name a company. Then I tell them that sticking with the status quo is too easy. "Doing nothing is probably your biggest competitor."

3. Priorities and Timing - "Do I have the time for this?"

Not every objection is about confusion or fear. Sometimes, it's about focus.

This is when you hear:

- *"This isn't a priority right now."*
- *"Let's revisit this in six months."*
- *"We have too much going on."*

Here's the reality; sometimes it's not an objection - it's simply the truth. People don't have time for everything, so they only focus on what feels urgent and critical, often what's top of mind for that quarter.

If your solution isn't sitting at the top of their priority list (top three minimum), then you've got no chance - you'll get pushed down the road and hear the classic, *"It's not a no, it's a not yet, lets speak again in 6 months"*

4. Budget and Business Constraints - "Can we even afford this?"

One of the most common objections is money. Prospects say things like:

- *"This is too expensive."*
- *"We don't have the budget for this right now."*
- *"We've already spent our budget on X instead."*

Sometimes, this is real - budget constraints and spending freezes do happen. More often though, this isn't about price; it's about value and the buyer not genuinely believing it works as well as you're saying.

Before MySalesCoach, I'd never spoken to a prospect who had what I sold as a line item on their budget spreadsheet. (With respect to MySalesCoach, it's not uncommon for a training budget to be set aside each year). Despite this, I've managed to sell time and time again; why? Because of the discovery, and aligning what we provided to a problem they had, and showing we could solve that problem and the impact of doing so through a business case.

5 - The One You Won't Like - [brace yourself]

You.

You, as the salesperson created it. You messed up. I told you that you wouldn't like it - it's an uncomfortable truth, but you can be the reason you get objections. Here are some examples of where salespeople tend to go wrong.

You didn't lead with the right problems, i.e. the ones they actually care about

If you're regularly hearing, *"We don't need this"* or *"This isn't a priority"*, you're either speaking to the wrong people or it's because you haven't connected your solution to an actual pain point.

You've either not done a deep enough discovery, made (poor) assumptions, asked ineffective questions, got happy ears and/or skipped ahead and jumped into pitching features and benefits.

You confused them

A confused mind doesn't buy. If a prospect is asking, 'Wait, how does this actually work?' or 'I don't see why we need this,' you probably weren't clear enough. Using too much technical jargon or sharing too many features and widgets is often the mistake I see here. Again, this is due to lack of discovery or a genuine understanding of their situation. When you lack that knowledge, you fail to connect their pain to your solution with real world examples and therefore rely on theoretical examples and explanations, using technical words and relying too much on features hoping one of them will resonate.

You shared the price too soon

If you're sharing price too early and hearing, "That's expensive" with no context as to the ROI then you've not discovered enough yet; you've been unable to build on pain, and the cost of inaction and have failed to convey the impact you can have. In this eventuality, the price will always feel too high.

One situation I do appreciate is the "direct prospect" who demands to know the price early. I used to push back and say, *"We'll get there"* I came to realise this was just creating unnecessary tension - it was making me seem like I had something to hide. Now, if I'm pushed early, I'll ask, *"Is buying something like this always going to be about price?"* Then I'll follow it up, but with ball park numbers and say something like, *"It's a little early to give an accurate price. There are a few things I'd need to know for sure, but my guess based on what I currently know is that the ballpark cost would be X-Y. Based on that, are you happy to continue?"*

You lost control

Losing control is almost always the result of not setting a good agenda. Control can be lost right after the small talk if you're not careful.

How can you tell if you've lost control?

They dictate, they say things like, *'Shall I tell you about us'*, *'Right, so give me the pitch'* and so forth. Another way you can tell is when you're stuck in question and answer mode (which will feel like objection and answer mode) and you are worrying that any time you say "No" to one of their questions, it will be game over.

You ignored the red flags

I've been that salesperson, I've heard something that would be deemed a red flag, but I've chosen to ignore it in fear of opening a can of worms. So silly of me. If a red flag is there, you're best to call it out early and know exactly where you stand. If you don't call them out now, they WILL come back and bite you further down the line. And by that point, you will have invested a lot of time into the deal.

Here are some examples of red flags I've ignored in the past that have come back to bite me:

- They asked about a feature we don't have, but I knew a competitor did. No surprise - they ended up buying from them because of that feature.

- They've not yet told their current provider they're leaving - shock, they re-signed. Time slipped away from them and it was easier to sign up for another year (no doubt having used me as a way to negotiate a better deal). But of course they'd be happy to speak in 12 months' time.
- They won't take you to power, they've "always got what they wanted" - shock, the CFO said no.
- They acknowledge the problem, but say it's not too bad - shock, they ghosted me.
- They told me results were dire and/or they're fed up working there - shock, they've "mutually decided" to move on.

When you hear a red flag, call it out. I actually call them red flags (sometimes I say orange) with something like this

"Happy to be told I'm wrong. I'm just sharing that I feel like I've heard a red flag in what you just said; when people ask about that feature it can be a deal breaker, is that the case for you?"

Again, don't fear the can of worms. Get to the truth. That's your job. The truth lets you invest your time in the right places and not waste it on deals that will never close.

Lack of trust

Trust is vital. A classic phrase in sales is, "People buy from people they like." I disagree. Of course, if you're not a nice person that will dramatically impact your success rate, but on the flip side, prospects can love you, and still not buy from you. I think a better phrase is, "People buy from people they trust". If they like you, it is a bonus.

Lack of trust can be the hardest one to accept, as it feels very personal. A lack of trust often results when:

- Their questions are being ignored or answered vaguely.
- The salesperson is just talking to them.
- They don't believe the answer they've been given is actually right for them.
- A salesperson talks too negatively about their current system or the competition.
- Responses feel too scripted or robotic.
- The salesperson is being overly pushy or aggressive.
- The salesperson is saying "yes" to everything.

In my experience trust is most often eroded through a small, consistent mix of the above and the good news is that they are avoidable behaviours when you learn the art of having conversations.

Lack of trust leads to objections like

- *How much experience does your company have in this industry?*
- *Have you worked with companies like ours before?*
- *What if we invest in this and it doesn't work?*
- *Do you have a case study that's exactly like our business?*
- *We'd have to run a pilot before we committed to anything.*

Building trust isn't just about having the right answers. It's about how you handle the conversation, how you position yourself, and whether you make the prospect feel like they're in good hands.

In summary, objections aren't the problem - silence is. The worst discovery calls aren't the ones where prospects push back; they're the ones where they nod along, disengaged, just waiting for it to be over. Objections mean your prospect is thinking, questioning, and giving you a chance to shift their perspective. If you're not hearing any, they've probably already decided it's a no and they're just too polite to say it outright. Knowing where objections come from, why they happen, and how to handle them isn't just a skill - it's what separates the best salespeople from those who are just going through the motions.

The most common objections you're likely to face

Objections might feel unpredictable, but the reality is most of them fall into a handful of categories. When you've been running discovery calls long enough, you start to notice the same patterns. Different words, different phrasing, but the same underlying concerns.

Most objections fit into one of these categories:

- **We already have something** - "We're already using X."
- **Features** - "Does it do [specific thing]?"
- **Adoption** - "I'm not sure the team will use it."
- **Timing/Priorities** - "Now's not the right time."

- **Comparison** - "Who are your competitors?"
- **Pricing** - "This is too expensive."
- **Non-committal** - "Send me some info, and I'll get back to you."

Let's break these down and look at what they actually mean, how a prospect brings them up, and when they do - what you really need to understand.

We already have something - "We're already using X."

This is the classic status quo objection. The prospect isn't necessarily saying no, they're saying they don't see a big enough reason to change.

Common ways a prospect brings this up:

- "We're already working with [competitor]. Switching systems would be a real headache."
- "We do this in-house, it's similar to what we're already doing."

What they actually mean:

- They are comfortable with what they have and they don't see why switching would be worth the time, effort, and money.
- They don't want to go through the hassle of change unless there's a major reason to do so.
- They aren't convinced your solution is significantly better than what they already use.

Key thing to uncover:

Are they truly happy with their current set-up, and thus never likely to leave, or is there frustration of any kind with what they're currently doing or who they're working with?

Key things to ask:

Try this: *"Of course, I expected you to have something in place. Just so I understand, when you evaluate your current provider, would you say it's perfect, or is there anything that could be better?"*

If they say it's perfect, the timing isn't right. But most prospects feel uncomfortable fully committing to that answer. You're more likely to hear something like *"I wouldn't go that far."*

From there, dig in.

- "How do you mean?"
- "What could be better?"

The information you gather here will help you position your product or service perfectly.

Features - "Does it do [specific thing]?"

A prospect hyper-focusing on features is rarely just about functionality. It's usually a sign that they don't fully understand the bigger picture yet or that you're being compared "like for like" with another system. And that doesn't mean it's a fair comparison - plenty of times, I've seen a product compared to a totally different system.

Common ways a prospect brings this up:

- "Does it integrate with [tool]?"
- "Can it do [very niche function]?"
- "How does this compare to [competitor] on X?"

What they actually mean:

- They don't know enough to evaluate this properly, so they're zooming in on one specific thing.
- They need to justify this internally and think this feature is a deal-breaker.
- They are trying to compare this to another solution but don't know how else to differentiate them.

Key thing to uncover:

Is this feature truly essential, or are they using it as a crutch to avoid making a decision? You need to ask questions that help you understand if it's truly essential and why.

Key things to ask:

- *"What will having that feature enable you to do, and how will you use it?"*
- *"Is this something you'd use regularly, or more of a 'nice to have'?"*

Try to figure out if this is a must-have feature that drives key outcomes or just something a competitor has sold them on that they'll never actually use. If it's a must-have and you don't have it, you're best saying so now.

Adoption - "I'm not sure the team will use it."

This is an adoption risk objection. Your prospect is worried about investing in something their team won't actually use.

Common ways a prospect brings this up:

- "We don't have the bandwidth to take this on."
- "We've tried something similar before, and it didn't work."
- "We'd need to run a POC before we could commit."

What they actually mean:

- If they push this forward and no one uses it, they'll look bad.
- They've tried new tools before, and they just sat there collecting dust, which didn't go down well with the CFO.
- This sounds good in theory, but they don't know if their team will care enough to change - or if they, as the manager, care enough to use it themselves.

Key thing to uncover:

Do they know the team won't use it, or are they just worrying that will be the case?

Key things to ask:

"Just so I understand, do you know that to be true, or do you think that to be true?"

Most people will not commit to "knowing" so they will say they think it's true. Now you can unpack it.

- "Why do you feel that way?"
- "Is that across the team, or just certain people?"

Maybe those not using it wouldn't because your proposed offering would force them to work in a better, more structured way. That could be a bigger issue - but one that will sink your deal if it is not addressed early.

If they *know* it's true, ask:

- "What previous experience has proven that?"
- "What could you learn from that past experience in order to change it this time?"
- And more importantly - do they even want to?

Timing/Priorities - "Now's not the right time."

The timing objection is often the easiest one for prospects to throw out because it's not a hard no, but it also doesn't commit them to anything.

Common ways a prospect brings this up:

- "Let's look at this again in six months."
- "We have too much going on right now."

What they actually mean:

- This isn't high on their priority list right now.
- They don't feel enough pain to make this urgent.
- They aren't convinced this is a better use of their time than the other things they are working on.

- Maybe they are not sure they'll be in that role much longer.

Key thing to uncover:

Are they genuinely too busy, or do they just not see the urgency?

Key things to ask:

"Just so I understand, what needs to change for this to become a priority?"

This should help you determine how realistic it is that this will ever be important to them

Comparison - "Who are your competitors?"

When a prospect asks about competitors, it's usually a sign they are either shopping around and haven't yet seen a clear differentiator, or looking for validation that they are making the right choice.

Common ways a prospect brings this up:

- "Who are your competitors?"
- "Why should we pick you over [competitor]?"
- "How do you compare to [competitor]?"

What they actually mean:

- They aren't sure what makes you different.
- They need to justify this choice to their boss.

Key thing to uncover:

Are they genuinely evaluating your offer, or are they just using this as an excuse to delay making a decision?

Key things to ask:

Spin it back on them and find out how they're going to decide. My talk track in these situations is:

"It depends how you're evaluating us. What do you need to see and know to be sure you've picked the right provider?"

This will normally give you some insight into how they're thinking. Typically, you'll hear things like:

- **Case studies/referrals/speaking with a customer** - They need social proof.
- **Price** - They're cost-sensitive, but are they just looking for the cheapest option?
- **Feature/report comparison** - They're focused on functionality, but what's the real driver?
- **Solving a specific problem** - They don't yet believe you can.

Once I understand their thinking, I'll reply:

"That's helpful. So based on that, I'd say our biggest competitor is actually 'do nothing.' It's always easier to stick with the status quo - perhaps you feel that way too?"

Let them justify why they wouldn't do anything. What's the pain of inaction, why can't this wait another six months?

Often, this is enough. If they need a competitor name, I'll give them one, along with a genuine compliment on what they do well. But the thing I highlight as a competitor's strength will always be something I know won't solve their problem.

Pricing - "This is too expensive."

The price objection is rarely about price itself - it's about value. If a prospect believes something is essential, or will make their life easier, better or more successful, then they'll find the money for it. If they don't believe that, no price will ever seem reasonable.

Common ways a prospect brings this up:

- "What's the ROI?"
- "This is a lot more than I expected."
- "We don't have the budget for this right now."

What they actually mean:

- They don't see the ROI clearly enough.
- They don't have the internal influence to justify this spend.
- They don't actually know how to buy it internally.

Key thing to uncover:

Are they actually price-sensitive, or do they just not see enough value yet?

Key things to ask:

"What's the ROI?"

"When it comes to ROI, help me understand how you would look to measure it."

Or try this *"Let's imagine we're here in 12 months, and your renewal is up - what would you need to have seen happen to make this a no-brainer?"*

This gets them thinking beyond the sale, imagining working with you. Now, you can sell them that vision using their words.

"This is a lot more than I expected."

When they have a price expectation, you need to understand what's given them that expectation.

"When you say 'expected,' what are you comparing it with?"

This helps you figure out whether they're evaluating the offer fairly and whether this is really about price or just a knee-jerk reaction.

A common issue here is personal perception of money as opposed to a business perception of money.

- For example, to most people, £20,000 is a lot of money.
- But to a business with a problem worth 10x that, it's not expensive at all if the impact is clear.

Sometimes, you need to help your prospect separate how they personally feel about the cost from how the business sees it.

"We don't have the budget for this right now."

You need to understand if this is a spending freeze (i.e., no one's buying anything for any reason) or if they could buy but it would take some effort (i.e., getting internal buy-in, building a business case).

Ask them:

"When people say there's no budget, it can mean different things. Is this a case of a spending freeze, or is it more that there's no set budget, but if you believed this would solve X problem, it would just be a case of putting together a business case?"

Non-committal - "Send me some info, and I'll get back to you."

This is a polite way of saying they aren't ready to engage yet.

Common ways a prospect brings this up:

- "Can you just send me some information?"
- "I wouldn't want to involve my boss yet."
- "Let me digest this and get back to you."

What they actually mean:

- They don't want to say no outright, so they're stalling.
- They don't feel in control of the process.

- They don't want to bring in their boss because they aren't convinced yet - or because their boss doesn't even know this problem exists.

Key thing to uncover:

Is this a genuine step in their process, or are they just trying to get you off the call?

Key things to ask:

"Can you send some information?"

"Happy to send something over. What do you need to see specifically?"

Then follow up with:

"Sure, if I take some time to put that together and send it over tomorrow, how long would you like to review it?"

Once they tell you that, suggest a follow-up call based on that timeframe. This is hard to say no to. They asked for info, you agreed, and accepted it will take time, so now it's only fair they agree to a follow-up.

"I don't want to involve the decision-maker yet."

You need to understand why.

"Sure, no wrong answers - just so I understand, what's the reason you'd be reluctant to include them at the next stage?"

By framing it as *"no wrong answers"*, you make it easier for them to justify their statement. Based on their response, you can decide whether to push again or not.

Tip: If your prospect is the champion or user, make sure they have seen a demo before you go to the decision-maker.

Once they've had the demo and you've learnt what's important to them, you use that in the next meeting (with the decision-maker) and get your champion to sell for you:

- "[Champion], you loved this feature - how does it compare to what you're doing now?"
- "[Champion], remind me, what would be the big win here if you had this?"
- "[Champion], what's the main reason you wanted to explore this in the first place?"

Summary

While objections might come in different forms, they nearly always boil down to the same core concerns. Whether it's uncertainty, risk, priorities, comparison, price, or a lack of commitment, your job isn't to "overcome" them - it's to understand what's really behind them. A surface-level objection is rarely the full picture. The best salespeople don't just answer questions, they ask the right ones back. They don't get defensive or rush to pitch; they stay curious, uncover the real hesitation, and guide the prospect toward a decision. Handle objections well, and you're not just keeping a deal alive - you're also proving your value before they've even bought. You're persuading them to see you as a trusted advisor.

The Mindset Shift: From Overcoming to Understanding

Most sales reps are conditioned to believe that objections are hurdles they need to "overcome." They hear an objection and go straight into challenge mode - trying to push back, prove a point, or convince the prospect they're wrong. I used to do it myself. I thought I was being clever when I'd say things like, *"How do you know you can't afford it yet? I haven't even told you the price."* In reality, I just sounded like an idiot and wound the prospect up. My toes were actually curling as I typed what I used to say.

The knee-jerk reaction to objections is the same as it is to questions - we must answer them, (and with objections we usually answer them defensively). It's just how we're wired; let me prove it:

- When was the Battle of Hastings?
- What's the capital of France?
- What's 2+2?
- Who sings "Shake it Off"?

If you know the answers you instinctively want to answer. That urge to respond kicks in automatically. In sales, that can work against you. The moment you rush to answer an objection, you miss the most important part: understanding *why* the prospect asked the question in the first place.

This is why new reps often do well in their first few months. They don't have all the answers yet, so they instinctively ask more questions.

For example

Prospect: "Does your system integrate with Salesforce?"
Seller: "When you say integrate, how do you mean?" "What are you hoping it does?"

Prospect: "Who are your competitors?"
Seller: "What's important to you when evaluating providers?" "Have you spoken to anyone else?"

Prospect: "Do you work with anyone like us?"
Seller: "Like you in what way? Industry, size, revenue, or the same challenge?"

Unfortunately that period is short-lived, once a rep is ramped and builds their knowledge bank, something changes. They stop asking. Instead, they start telling.

Prospect: "Does your system integrate with Salesforce?"
Seller: "Yes, it does, and it also has a XYZ feature."

Prospect: "Who are your competitors?"
Seller: "We have a few, namely ABC."

Prospect: "Do you work with anyone like us?"
Seller: "Yeah, I can send over some case studies."

The seller hears a question and immediately jumps in with an answer, thinking they're being helpful. But all they've done is take a surface-level question at face value, missing the chance to learn why the prospect is asking in the first place.

The elite salespeople? They know the answers - however they still act like the newbie. They still ask questions first.

Prospect: "Does your system integrate with Salesforce?"
Seller: "Tell me more - what have you got in mind? Why's that important to you? How would that help?"

Prospect: "Who are your competitors?"
Seller: "Interesting - have you spoken with anyone else yet? What are you looking for in a supplier?"

"Doing nothing is actually a big one - most companies stick with the status quo. Is that what you were thinking?"

Prospect: "Do you work with anyone like us?"
Seller: "Companies like yours in what way? What metric are you referring to?"

Objections can often be answered with a question. And by doing that, you uncover the real reason behind them.

Newbies and top performers both keep asking questions. The ones in between - the reps who've been in place for 6 to 24 months, are often the ones who jump to conclusions, give answers too quickly, and add more detail than necessary. They think they're moving the deal forward; in reality, they're learning nothing.

The best sellers don't focus on overcoming objections. They focus on understanding them. Because once you understand what's really going on, you don't need to "overcome" anything - you just need to help the prospect get to the right decision.

How to handle objections - The PAUA framework

So far we've covered what objections are, why we get them, what they mean, questions to ask in response and the mindset shift needed from overcoming them to understanding them. But knowing all of that is one thing - handling an objection in the moment, when the pressures on, is another.

This is where most reps slip up. They hear an objection and react instantly. Either they get defensive - "That's not really an issue because X", they give a weak answer that even they don't believe, or they rush in with a counterargument, trying to shut it down.

Either way, it all feels rushed. The best salespeople slow things down. They don't rush to fix the objection or treat it as something to bulldoze through. Instead, they take control of the moment, process what's actually being said, and respond in a way that moves the conversation forward.

The key is to have a simple, repeatable way of handling objections - something you can fall back on in real time without overthinking it. That's where the PAUA framework comes in.

I know what you're thinking, another framework. Everyone's got one. But like most of them, the value isn't in the name - it's in having a rhythm, this framework is a structured way to handle objections properly instead of knee-jerking your way through them.

The best reps handle objections with active listening, empathy, and a focus on whether there's actually a path forward. The PAUA framework makes sure you do exactly that.

It stands for: Pause. Acknowledge. Understand. Ask.

Pause

Do exactly that. Pause. Do nothing. Count to two in your head. Stay silent. Use that silence to show you're thinking.

This alone stops you from reacting on autopilot; it also gives the prospect space to keep talking. If you just let the silence hang in the air for a second, you'll be amazed how often they'll fill the silence and clarify, or even soften their own objection.

Acknowledge

People like to feel heard - show them you've heard them, acknowledge what they've said.

- "Yeah, I hear that a lot."
- "That makes sense."
- "Interesting, I can see the reason you've asked that."

If you don't acknowledge it and jump in defensively, you set the alarm bells ringing and start to erode the trust.

Understand

To understand you need to ask a question that unpacks what they've said. As mentioned previously, objections are rarely about what's said on the surface. "We don't have the budget" could mean there's no money, or it could mean they don't see enough value. "We use a competitor" might mean they love them, or it might mean they're open to switching if there's a strong reason. You don't know unless you ask. It's your job to know, you have to get to the truth.

Ask

Once you've paused, acknowledged and understood you're able to make a case that there could still be a path forward; you do that with a small ask.

At this point it's clear, you're not trying to overcome the objection, you've understood it correctly. Now you're simply figuring out if there's still a next step or it's game over.

Since it's a small ask, the next step - if suitable - should feel logical, whether it's exploring the problem further, getting them to think differently, or setting up another conversation. Keep it small, and keep it logical.

What this looks like in practice with a real example

Context: David is a sales manager. "He has a full quota and two brand new SDRs they've hired fresh out of University. He asked me for a call. The call lasted 50 minutes and, when it came to the price, this is what he said

David: *"Look, I'm sold this is exactly what we need but there's no budget for this, getting this approved will be a big internal challenge; the business will see this as a big expense"*

In truth, I was STUNNED that he said this. I was proposing a £3.5K coaching package for each SDR. Here's just some of the things that had been mentioned on the call

- David had explicitly said that his SDRs needed coaching and that he didn't have the time or ability to do this himself.

- There was a finite window in which to get them ramped. He had two months to solve this problem.
- The cost of doing nothing was "massive" (his words) as the cost was estimated to be over £100k.
- This wasn't a "nice to have", they'd hired 2 SDRS to do outbound sales and, as they had hired graduates, they knew they lacked the skills necessary to do the job.

Given what I knew, it would have been SO easy for me to jump in here, with a knee jerk reaction and say something like;

- It's only £3,500 per person, surely you can afford that given the business case?
- If you don't invest in their development you might as well fire them, they won't be successful without MySalesCoach.
- Why do you need to ask for approval for such a small amount?
- You won't find a better price for what we can do.
- You've only got two months to act, and the cost of doing nothing will be massive.

An untrained salesperson would turn to pressure and urgency tactics; in the process, they'd have sounded salesy and lost their trust and credibility.

Instead I used the PAUA framework.

I **Paused** for two seconds...

I **Acknowledged** him.

Me: *"I hear you, it's rare you hire salespeople and have an immediate coaching budget set aside. That will potentially make for an internal challenge to get this signed off and be seen as a big, additional expense"*

I then tried to **Understand** him

"Just so I understand, when I hear there's no budget and internal challenges around sign-off it can mean one of two things, the first is "This is a non-starter; despite the predicament I'm in there's nothing we can do." The second is more you managing my expectations, to show me that while you want to move forward I should expect to speak with other stakeholders who we may need to take on a bit of a journey as to why they need this and even put together a business case - which one are you?"

David: "It's the second one for sure, I've not purchased something like this before and I know they will say it is my job to coach them, but I know that's not going to work"

Then I made a small **Ask**

"Given you and I want the same thing, to work together, and that we both feel there's a business case here even if it is perhaps not quite solid enough to put in front of your CFO YET, should we speak again? Time has run away today but we can have another call and use that time to create a solid business case together and discuss how we best present this to the CFO"

David "Yes, let's do that, that's a good idea."

The PAUA framework worked perfectly here. Why? Because I didn't see it as a conflict between David and me. I actually saw us both on the same side of the negotiation table. We wanted the same thing, so I paused, gave it some thought, acknowledged what he had to say, and then dug into his logic by understanding it.

It was now clearer to me he didn't know how to buy. I then made a small ask that ultimately said I heard the objection, but despite that there was still a path forward. So my suggestion of another call felt entirely logical and easy to buy into.

This is a very different approach to the examples I gave from a typical salesperson. The PAUA framework isn't about fighting them and telling them while they're wrong, but it's also not just blindly accepting the objection. By using this approach I'm keeping the conversation open and seeing if there's actually a deal to be done.

Here's another example

Context: Sarah is a VP of Sales at a fast-growing SaaS company. She'd been in her role for six months, and her biggest challenge was that her Account Executives were struggling to close mid-market deals. They were getting strong interest in demos, but deals kept stalling before contracts got signed.

She reached out to me for a conversation. We discussed her team's process, the roadblocks they were hitting, and what she'd already tried to fix it. We agreed that 1:1 coaching for each person would be incredibly helpful; by the time we got to the end of the call, she was nodding along, saying everything made sense.

And then, like clockwork, came the objection.

Sarah: *"I really like this, but I think in all honesty we need to fix some internal processes first before we bring in 1:1 coaching."*

If I wasn't disciplined, I could have gone straight into convincing mode:

- *"Coaching will actually help fix those internal processes faster."*
- *"That's exactly why we should start now."*
- *"But Sarah, if you wait, you're going to continue losing more deals."*

While all of these points were true, if I fired them back too quickly, I would have sounded like I was dismissing her concern and trying to push her towards my agenda, rather than working with her to solve it.

Instead, I used PAUA:

Pause

I let the silence sit for two seconds. No rush to react. No immediate response. Just giving her space.

Acknowledge

Me: *"That makes sense. When internal processes are being reviewed, people can lean this way. After all, it* can feel like a mistake to add something new when the foundations aren't solid yet."

I could tell that she felt understood by the way she looked at me. I didn't try to debate her logic with her. I didn't tell her why I thought she was wrong. Instead I told her that other people feel the same way, I kept the conversation consultative and, most importantly, alive.

Understand

Me: *"Just so I understand, when you say you need to fix internal processes first, do you mean things like messaging and playbooks, or do you mean structural issues, like who's on the team or the way the team manages the sales process?"*

Sarah: *"It's more about our sales process - we have a lot of inconsistency between the way reps are running their discovery calls, demos and follow-ups, and I don't want to layer coaching on top of a broken system."*

That was useful information. If I'd jumped straight into convincing mode, I wouldn't have got this level of detail. Now I knew that 1:1 coaching might not be the best way we could help; instead we might be able to do something with the team as a group and provide baseline training and coaching.

Ask

Me: *"That makes a lot of sense... Just thinking out loud here - if part of the problem is inconsistency and it's across the team, then rather than 1:1 coaching from the start, what if we looked to do something with the group as a whole, a focussed group coaching programme that covered discovery, demo and follow-up. That would mean that, instead of everyone doing their own thing, they'd all be on the same page"*

Sarah: *"That's a really interesting idea; tell me more."*

Boom. The conversation was still alive and we had a better understanding of her needs and how we could help.

I could have gone straight into convincing mode, but instead, I made sure Sarah felt heard. The moment a prospect feels like you're pushing them into something, they instinctively push back. By acknowledging her concern rather than arguing against it, I kept the conversation open rather than turning it into a debate.

I asked a question that got Sarah to clarify her real concern.

Sarah's initial objection sounded like a generic "not yet," but when I asked her to clarify, she revealed that the real issue wasn't just about processes - it was inconsistency across the team. If I'd pushed for 1:1 coaching, I'd have been solving the wrong problem.

I didn't just sell - I co-created a solution with her.

Instead of forcing my original idea, I pivoted and suggested something that actually made more sense based on what she had told me. This made it feel like we were working *together* rather than me trying to sell her something. Prospects don't like feeling like they're being sold to, but they do like feeling like they're making smart decisions.

I made a small ask that kept the conversation moving.

I didn't say, "Let's sign up today." I didn't pressure her into making a big commitment. I simply suggested an alternative that aligned with what she wanted, and I let her come to the conclusion herself. The result? Instead of shutting the conversation down, she said: *"That's a really interesting idea, tell me more."*

This is another example of why the **PAUA** works. It stopped me from going into defensive mode, it stopped me from sounding salesy, and, most importantly it helped me uncover a better fit for Sarah's needs, positioned me as a trusted advisor and gave us a path forward.

Dealing with multiple objections at once

Often, objections don't come one at a time, they're stacked and delivered in one go. This was something said to me recently

"We don't have budget, I'm not sure all of the team would use it, and feel like we should be using our enablement team more"

When that happens, the worst thing you can do is panic and try to answer everything at once. That just turns into a messy back-and-forth where nothing really gets resolved. Here's what I said, after the pause, of course.

"Okay, you've thrown a few things at me there"

They laughed.

"Let me go through and make sure I understand each of these one at a time, I think I've got all of them written down but, if at the end you think I've missed anything, just call it out, okay? Okay, so the first thing is budget"

And from there I went through my normal routine, of acknowledging, understanding and then making an ask to see if there was still a path forward.

"Okay, the next thing was not being convinced all of the team would use it."

And so forth

This approach works because it does three things really well:

It slows the conversation down.

When a prospect stacks multiple objections, it's usually a sign that they're either feeling overwhelmed or unsure. If you jump straight into rapid-fire responses, you add to the chaos. Instead, pausing and saying "Okay, you've thrown a few things at me there" immediately takes the tension out of the moment. It makes it a bit light hearted as well it reminds them that you too are a human being and they've just thrown a load of stuff at you. This also gives you control and makes the conversation feel more structured rather than a messy back-and-forth.

It makes them feel heard.

People don't just want answers - they want to feel understood. Saying "Let me go through and make sure I understand each of these, one at a time" shows that you're listening properly, not just waiting for your turn to speak. That small moment of laughter or a smile? That's them realising you're not rattled, and more importantly, you're not treating this as an argument you need to win.

It stops objections from reinforcing each other.

When a prospect rattles off multiple objections at once, they're building a case against moving forward. If you try to tackle them all in one go, you risk making their doubts even stronger. By breaking them down one by one, you isolate each concern, stopping them from feeding into each other. More often than not, once you've properly addressed the first objection, the others start to lose their weight.

This approach keeps you in control, keeps the conversation open, and ensures nothing gets lost in the noise. Instead of scrambling to overcome objections, you methodically work through them - keeping the prospect engaged and leading them towards a real decision.

When to walk away

The best salespeople don't just know how to handle objections - they know which ones to handle and which ones to walk away from. Elite salespeople don't waste time trying to win over people who were never going to buy in the first place.

Here's when to recognise you're better off giving up.

They don't actually have the problem you solve: Walk away. No amount of pitching, persuasion, or clever objection handling is going to sell someone something they don't need. If they truly don't have the pain point, move on.

They're just gathering quotes as part of their due diligence: Walk away (or reset the conversation). If they only care about price, they're probably benchmarking you to get a better deal with their current or preferred supplier. Instead of playing along, challenge it early: *"When price is the main driver, it typically means one of two things, one is that you're doing this because your boss has told you to just check other prices before proceeding or because you have a preferred supplier, you just want to try and negotiate a better price by seeing what others charge. Is something like that happening here?"*. If they won't engage in a real conversation and just want a price, they're not worth chasing.

They're resistant to engaging at all: Walk away. If they won't answer your questions, won't tell you their buying process, and won't share what's important to them, take the hint. You can't close a deal when the prospect won't engage in a conversation.

The Importance of disqualifying early: I learnt this lesson far too late in my career. "Spend your time with people who want to buy" I used to be such a hopeful salesperson, hoping every deal would close. Only when a coach told me this did I realise I needed to qualify out more than I was doing. A huge part of selling is knowing when not to sell. The best reps aren't just great at handling objections - they're also ruthless at disqualifying bad deals early. They don't let hope cloud reality. Every minute you spend chasing the wrong prospect is a minute you should be spending with the right one.

Key Takeaways

Objections aren't obstacles you need to "overcome." They're signals. They tell you what your prospect is thinking, what's holding them back, and what they actually care about. If you treat them as something to fight against, you'll always have friction with your prospect. If you treat them as a chance to understand, you'll be the one seller they actually trust.

The goal isn't to counter every objection with a perfect rebuttal. It's to get to the truth. Why is your prospect hesitating? What's their real concern? What would need to change for them to move forward? The best salespeople don't try to "win" every objection. Instead, they uncover what truly matters, address it properly, and, when necessary, they know when to walk away.

At the end of the day, selling isn't about forcing a decision. It's about making sure the right decision gets made. Shift from overcoming to understanding, and you'll stop "selling" - instead, you'll start guiding. And that's when real deals happen.

Chapter Nine

The Difficult Prospect

Let's face it. Not every prospect we hop on a call with is going to be friendly, forthcoming with information, and ready to answer the questions we want to ask them. Life would be easy if that were true!

You've probably had experience of dealing with the following types of prospects:

- Prospects who seem determined to make the conversation as challenging as possible.
- Prospects who are guarded and reluctant to share information.
- Prospects who appear confrontational or as if they don't want to be on the call with you.
- Prospects who appear distracted or even stressed.

Difficult prospects can derail a discovery call before it even starts. But the best sales professionals don't just survive these interactions; they turn them into opportunities. They know that resistance sometimes signals underlying pain, skepticism, or past bad experiences with salespeople. Instead of retreating or pushing harder, they lean in with curiosity, patience, and a strategic approach.

Difficult prospects can still become great customers - it all comes down to communication and trust.

This chapter will equip you with the tools to navigate tough conversations with confidence. You'll learn how to break down walls, reset the tone of a call, and turn disengagement into meaningful dialogue. It will enable you to learn when a prospect is there to be "won over" and when it may instead be the right thing to pull the plug on the conversation.

I will give examples of different types of challenging situations, along with real transcripts from my own conversations:

The prospect who says, "Just give me a demo"

This is a situation we have probably all been in before. The prospect doesn't want to answer any of your "discovery questions," just to see the product. Here's a real transcript in which this happened:

1. Handling Pushback and Setting the Frame

> **Prospect:** *"Listen, I know you want to ask me your questions, but can we just cut to the chase and you show me the product?"*

> **Me:** *"I totally understand you're busy, and I want to be respectful of your time. I'll make sure you see the product today. I could jump straight into the demo, but I've found that, if I did that without*

some quick context, we'd probably be here for three hours if I ran through every feature from the top. So to make sure this is valuable for you, can you give me a sense of what made you interested in seeing the product in the first place?"

Why This Works:

- **Acknowledge their request -** This validates their concern to avoid pushback.
- **Provide a logical reason for asking questions** - This positions discovery as a way to save time, not slow things down.
- **Ask a low-friction question** - This shifts the conversation without sounding forceful.

2. Uncovering the Business Context

Prospect: *"We're exploring options. I want to see if this is better than what we have now."*
Me: *"Got it. And when you purchased your current solution, what problem were you looking to solve?"*

Why This Works:

- **Gently redirect the situation from "better" to "problem-solving"** - This helps the prospect articulate what's missing.
- **Encourage them to reflect on past decisions** - This exposes any gaps between expectations and reality.

3. Isolating Key Pain Points

> **Prospect:** *"We wanted a tool to help us coach our reps to have better sales conversations and share best practices."*

> **Me:** *"That makes sense. And what's missing or frustrating about your current solution that's making you shop around? If I can understand that, I'll focus on what actually matters to you in a quick overview demo."*

Why This Works:

- **Confirm their response before digging deeper** - This keeps the conversation natural.
- **Frame the question as helpful, not intrusive** - This puts the prospect in control while steering the discussion toward pain points.

4. Pinpointing the Switching Motivations and Gaining Buy-In

> **Prospect:** *"Well, our current tool has had lots of complaints from the sales team about ease of use. It's difficult to share great examples, and its coaching features are weak."*

> **Me:** *"Got it. So usability and coaching features. Those are two things we find a lot of teams switch to us for. Let me show you how we approach that, and you can tell me if it's a fit."*

Why This Works:

- **Summarise key pain points concisely** - This shows active listening and ensures alignment.
- **Use social proof** - This reinforces the idea that others have switched for the same reasons, reducing perceived risk.
- **Position the demo as a solution, not just a walkthrough** - This keeps the prospect engaged while maintaining control.

This approach ensures the demo is relevant by shifting the conversation from a generic product tour to a value-driven discussion, keeping the prospect engaged without creating friction.

The prospect who says "I can't even remember what this call is about"

Some prospects take the call but have completely forgotten why they booked it in the first place. It can thus derail the conversation if you immediately try to pitch or ask detailed questions they aren't mentally prepared for. Instead of making them feel unprepared, I take control by resetting the tone, reframing the problem we solve, and confirming it's still relevant to them before moving forward. Here is a real example of this happening to me:

Resetting the Tone and Taking Control

> **Prospect:** *"I'm gonna be honest. I can't even remember what this call is about. Can you just remind me what it is you guys do?"*

Me: *"No worries at all. I know how packed your calendar must be and I did call you out of the blue. To jog your memory, when we first connected, we talked about how sales leaders often lack the time or bandwidth to coach their sellers, but ultimately know that there are specific skills or behaviours they are lacking and this is holding them back from hitting ambitious targets. On the initial call you mentioned that the bit about lacking time to coach struck a chord. Does that sound familiar?"*

Prospect: "Yeah OK, it does ring a bell now and the stuff around lack of time to coach is something that I've been experiencing a lot recently..."

Why This Works:

- **Keep it casual and low-pressure** - This acknowledges their busy schedule without making them feel unprepared.
- **Reframe the conversation around their pain, not my product** - This positions the call as relevant by focusing back on the initial reason why they agreed to the call, even if they forgot why they booked it.
- **Asks for confirmation** - This invites them to re-engage without pushing too hard.

This method turns an awkward start into an engaging, problem-focused discussion, keeping the prospect invested.

The prospect who says "We're working with your competitor, I just want to see what else is out there"

Some prospects take a call not because they're seriously considering switching, but because they want leverage in a renewal negotiation. The challenge here is to quickly determine:

1. Are they just price-shopping? If so, I don't waste time chasing a deal that won't happen.
2. Are they genuinely looking for a better solution? If so, you need to uncover the real reason they're considering switching.

The key is to stay curious, test their commitment to their existing vendor, and focus on what's driving them to explore alternatives.

Resetting the Tone and Qualifying Their Intent

> **Prospect:** *"We're working with [competitor], I just want to see what else is out there."*

> **Me:** *"Got it. That's helpful to know. Out of curiosity, what's prompting you to explore other options now?"*

- Keep it neutral - Don't react emotionally or jump into a pitch.
- Put the ball in their court - If they're serious, they'll reveal their motivation.

Testing Their Commitment to Their Existing Vendor

> **Prospect:** *"Oh, just making sure we're aware of all the options, and ultimately that we are getting the best deal from them".*

> **Me**: *"That makes sense. Most teams don't explore alternatives unless there's something they'd like to improve. But switching out technology comes with a lot of work and hassle for admins and users. Why not just negotiate a better deal with [competitor]? I'm sure they'd hate to lose you."*

- Force them to justify why they're looking - If they brush it off, they might just be price-shopping.
- Eliminate weak opportunities - If they have no real dissatisfaction, they'll probably admit it here.
- Increase credibility - Show that you're not desperate to win the deal - you only want real opportunities.

Filtering Out Price-Shoppers

> **Prospect**: *"Well, we're happy overall, but we want to see what's out there."*

> **Me**: *"Is it fair to say therefore that, if everything stays the same with [competitor], you are leaning toward staying with them?"*

- Directly test their willingness to switch - If they hesitate, I know there's a real pain point.

- Avoid being a pricing slave - If they confirm they're staying, I don't waste time chasing.

Digging Into Their Real Pain Points

Prospect: *"Actually, we do have some frustrations. It doesn't properly integrate with our CRM, and the transcription quality isn't great."*

Me: *"That's really helpful to hear. A lot of teams we speak with have struggled with [competitor] for similar reasons. What's been the ripple effects of the poor CRM integration and transcription for you?"*

- Get them to admit the real issue - Now you have a real reason they're looking.
- Use social proof strategically - Reinforces that others have switched for similar reasons.
- Dig into specifics - If they open up, you know they're more likely to switch.

This approach **separates serious buyers from those just fishing for a discount**, keeping me focused on real opportunities.

The prospect who appears distracted

Some prospects join a call but aren't mentally present. They show up late, look stressed, and spend more time staring at a second monitor than engaging in the conversation. When this happens, there are two choices:

1. **Push forward and hope to regain their attention** - which usually results in a disengaged, unproductive call.

2. **Acknowledge the situation directly** - giving them an easy out while maintaining control of the conversation.

Rather than fighting for their attention (the approach most salespeople will take), I take the second approach.

Resetting the Tone and Addressing the Distraction Directly

Me: *"I get the impression this call has just not come at a great time for you, Phil. No wrong answers, but would this be a more productive call if we spoke tomorrow instead?"*

- **Acknowledge reality without being confrontational** - Instead of pretending not to notice, call it out in a way that feels respectful, not accusatory.
- **Give them permission to reschedule** - This makes it easier for them to admit if they truly can't focus.
- **Retakes control** - Instead of passively accepting a distracted prospect, I steer the conversation toward a better outcome.

Possible Responses and How I Handle Them

Scenario 1: The Prospect Admits They're Too Busy

Prospect: *"Yeah, honestly, I'm swamped. Let's reschedule."*

Me: *"No problem at all - I'd rather talk when you can be fully engaged. How's tomorrow at [specific time]?"*

- **Lock in a new time immediately** - This avoids getting lost through, "Let's touch base later" territory.
- **Maintain control of scheduling** - I suggest a time instead of leaving it open-ended.

Scenario 2: The Prospect Insists on Continuing

Prospect: *"No, no it's fine, let's go ahead."*

Me: *"Are you sure? I want to make sure this is valuable for you."*

- **Give them a second chance to reschedule** - If they double down, they're more likely to stay engaged.
- **The prospect is more likely to be attentive -** Every time this has happened to me, the prospect has quickly changed their mentality and given the call their undivided attention. They simply feel more accountable now they know I have identified that they were distracted.

This method ensures that, when we do have a conversation, it's a productive one - not just another forgettable Zoom call. Having a quality conversation later is better than an unproductive conversation now.

The prospect who is a closed book

Some prospects make every question feel like an interrogation. They give short, guarded responses, so that pulling meaningful information from them feels like a struggle. More often than not, this isn't just their personality - it's a trust issue. They don't know you well enough to open up (yet).

If you keep pressing with direct discovery questions, it will just make them shut down further. I always remember a valuable sales lesson from a former mentor who told me that, in sales, we should always be looking to lower resistance. So, with this type of prospect, the key is to:

1. Acknowledge their guarded nature without making them defensive.
2. Lower their guard by shifting from "tough" questions to conversational ones.
3. Earn their trust by showing I understand their world before asking for deeper insights.

Resetting the Tone and Building Trust

Me: *"I get the sense you've had a few of these types of calls before, and you probably don't love answering a ton of questions from salespeople."*

- Call out the elephant in the room in a non-confrontational way - This shows you're self-aware, not just another pushy rep.
- Acknowledge their experience - Instead of forcing them to engage, validate the way they feel.
- Start breaking down resistance - People open up when they feel understood, not pressured.

Reframing the Conversation to Ease the Tension

Me: *"Totally fair. I don't want this to feel like an interrogation - I just want to make sure this is actually worth your time. From speaking with other CROs this year, a couple of things tend to be top of mind: The fact they need their AEs to self-generate more of their own pipeline, but also the fact that it's becoming harder for their salespeople to differentiate in super crowded categories. Do either of those sound familiar to you?"*

- Shift from asking to offering - Instead of forcing them to give me answers, I put ideas on the table for them to react to.
- Use pattern recognition - If they see their challenges reflected in what I share, they'll feel more comfortable engaging.
- I'm bringing in real examples from people they would associate as industry peers. People generally feel safer when they hear familiar challenges being shared from people just like them.
- Gives them an easier way to respond - A simple "yes" or "no" feels much safer than a broad, open-ended question.

Gradually Getting Them to Open Up

Prospect: *"Yeah, maybe a little of your first point."*

Me: *"Got it, that's helpful. Some of the specific things I'm seeing there is that, for many AEs, it is more of a mindset shift they need to make than anything else. They haven't had to cold call for years. Does that line up with what you're seeing, or is it different in your world?"*

- Mirror their energy - I don't pounce on their small admission; I ease into the conversation.
- Keep the conversation fluid - The "or is it different in your world?" makes it easier for them to engage without feeling locked in.
- Build momentum slowly - Each small confirmation helps lower their guard for deeper discussion.

This method ensures that, instead of forcing answers from a closed-book prospect, I gradually earn the right to have a real conversation

The prospect who keeps rescheduling

Some prospects genuinely have busy schedules. Others are just avoiding the conversation but don't want to outright cancel. Every reschedule means more time that you are sinking into potential wasted call preparation. And that is not to mention valuable slots on your calendar being wasted by cancelled meetings, which could have been replaced with genuine opportunities.

That's why I follow a "three strikes and you're out" approach:

1. First reschedule. No problem, life happens. I confirm the new date.
2. Second reschedule. I acknowledge the pattern and reschedule. Sometimes bad luck means meetings get pushed for the second time.
3. Third reschedule. I call it out directly and put the ball in their court.

If they keep pushing the meeting, I send the following email:

> Subject: Pull the plug?
>
> Graham – please correct me if I'm wrong here, but normally when people reschedule for the third time, it suggests that this conversation is likely terrible timing and exploring [X Problem] is just not a priority for you right now.
>
> Shall we pull the plug on this and reconvene later in the year?
>
> Rich

Why This Works:

- Call out the pattern directly - No sugarcoating.
- Reinforce the problem that piqued their interest - This reminds them as to why they agreed to the call in the first place.
- Trigger a response - If they are genuinely interested, this forces them to commit. If they're not, I move on without wasting more time.

This approach ensures I protect my time while maintaining professionalism and control

The prospect who is tight for time

Some prospects join a scheduled 30-minute call and immediately say:

"Just a heads-up, I've only got 10 minutes."

At this point, there are two choices:

1. Push forward and cram everything into 10 minutes - which rarely leads to a productive conversation.
2. Call it out and offer an alternative - ensuring we have a real discussion instead of a rushed one.

I take the second approach.

Resetting the Tone and Offering an Alternative

Prospect: *"Just a heads-up, I've only got 10 minutes."*

Me: *"No problem at all - I appreciate you letting me know. Ten minutes is going to fly by but I do want to be respectful of your time. Would it make more sense to find a more convenient time to have this conversation?"*

- Respect their time - No frustration, just a simple offer.
- Test their real level of interest - If they're serious, they'll reschedule. If they dodge, they probably aren't that motivated.

If They Say, "No, Let's Just Use the 10 Minutes"

Me: *"Got it. 10 minutes isn't a lot of time, so let's make this count. What's the one thing you were hoping to learn from this conversation?"*

- Call out the reality of the situation - Forces them to focus.
- Put the ball in their court - Ensures you can prioritise what's most important to them.

If They Engage and Show Interest

Me: *"That's helpful. I can give you a high-level answer now, but if this is something you're genuinely looking to solve, would you be open to carving out more time to explore it properly?"*

- Confirm their level of motivation - If they're just window shopping, I don't chase.
- Gain a soft commitment for a longer follow-up. If they see value, they'll find the time.

This approach ensures I have meaningful conversations, not just quick check-the-box calls.

So there you have it - some actionable approaches to dealing with different scenarios of difficult prospects. Remember though, HOW you sound when you respond is nearly as important as WHAT you say. Remain curious, measured, and non-confrontational. Practice your responses with a coach or colleague. Record yourself and listen back. This is critical to getting better as a salesperson.

Most reps see a difficult prospect as a roadblock. Top sellers see them as a challenge worth solving. The next time you're faced with one, will you default to frustration or take control of the conversation?

Chapter Ten

Who Really Makes the Decision?

I remember when I was in the early part of my sales career and I sat through some Sales 101 training. While most of the material was highly unmemorable, there was one thing I remember very clearly:

"Sell to the decision maker."

"Get access to the decision maker."

"Spend your time with decision makers."

So much importance was placed on the "decision maker". And it's a phrase which is ubiquitous in the world of sales.

The problem is that, over the years, the concept of "decision makers" has become so warped, that if you were to ask ten salespeople how they define a decision maker, you would probably get ten different answers.

These might include:

- The person who can authorise a purchase.
- The person who can make or break a deal.
- A person of influence.
- A person who has the authority to sign things off.
- Someone who can make things happen.

- People with power.
- People who can take you to people with power.

The reality is that all of the above can be true.

In the world of complex B2B sales, it would be fair to say that having one single decision maker in a deal is highly unusual.

Indeed, when I look back at some of the deals which I have closed over recent years, in some cases I had as many as 18 people involved in the discovery conversation!

That is why I think it's wrong to just think of a "decision maker" as a single person. While that may be true in more transactional sales, in a world where on average seven stakeholders are involved in a complex buying decision, you are being too narrow-minded if you believe that there is only one person making a decision.

This chapter is a practical playbook for navigating the real-world complexities of B2B sales, where deals aren't won by selling to one person but by winning over an entire buying committee.

If one person doesn't make the decision, then who really does? And more importantly, how do you engage with all of the people who truly hold influence in the deal?

To start with, let's look at the importance of accessing "power" in our deals:

The Importance of "Power"

Peeling it all back, the biggest issue I see many salespeople face in progressing deals is down to their inability to get access to power.

How do you define power?

In sales, power isn't just a job title - it's the ability to get things done. Power doesn't always sit with the person who signs the contract. It's the person who can move timelines, secure budgets, and influence others internally.

And when I think back to all of the deals that I have lost to either "no decision" or to the competition, a large proportion of those were down to the fact I was stuck with prospects who didn't have the ability to act or produce an effect.

So why is getting access to power so critical for sales success?

Power squashes timelines

I remember running a deal that was into its third month. My prospect, "the champion" was openly sharing pain and the reasons why they wanted to change. I also knew that we were their preferred vendor. But the deal was dragging. The problem I had was that I had yet to have a conversation with "power". In this case, that was the Chief Revenue Officer. By chance, I bumped into them at a networking event and struck up a conversation. Two weeks later and, after a scheduled post-event Zoom call, the deal was done.

It wasn't so much that this deal would never have happened had I not bumped into the CRO that evening. But ultimately, the moment that power got proactively involved, the deal accelerated at a rapid pace.

Power has the ability to accelerate decision making in a business. Given we all know that "time kills deals", power's ability to squash timelines ultimately de-risks your deals.

Power is comfortable talking about pain

If you have ever sold to junior prospects, you have probably found that they are not in their comfort zone talking about real business pain or the money required to fix such pain. Ultimately, this is the thing that gets companies to write cheques, so the quicker you get access to power the better. Power is less bogged down in company politics and preserving their own image. Their motivation to act is typically in the interests of the business (rather than their own).

Power qualifies in/out quicker

Since power has the ability to make or break a deal, as a seller, you know where you stand a lot quicker. Actually having somebody who can say no in a forthright way should be seen as a huge win as a seller. Think back to all of the time you have lost chasing deals over the years, simply because you were dealing with someone who didn't have the courage or authority to say "no". Time is our most precious commodity as sellers. Anything we can do to be spending it on our best deals should be fiercely embraced.

Power can get deals done

In light of the dictionary definition of "the ability to act", power has a funny way of getting deals done. A key point here is that this doesn't necessarily mean they will sign a contract or authorise an expenditure. But they certainly have the nous and credibility to get others to do so.

Why We Fail

Before we look at the tactical side of how to access power in our discovery process, it's important to acknowledge *why* we fail to get access to power.

You are nervous about offending your champion

Many sellers feel nervous about offending their champion by asking to go above their head. It's understandable - especially when some prospects are simply protective of their own power.

You don't understand your prospect's true problems

It may sound obvious, but when your prospect feels like you haven't understood their true problems or business challenges, then you will have failed to build trust with them. When there is no trust, then there is no hope of them giving you access to power.

If all you ever do is get stuck talking about surface level problems and "nice to solve" issues with prospects, then they aren't going to take you to people who spend their days tackling BIG business problems that they MUST solve.

You aren't high up on their list of priorities

This is somewhat connected to the previous point, but here's a tough pill to swallow:

If the problem you can solve is not at least in the top three priorities of the prospect you are selling to, then there is a very low chance of them buying. This was a tough thing for me to accept when I learned it, as I suddenly realised half of my pipeline was probably dead meat.

You need to get your prospect to tell you that you are high on the list. If you're not, then you won't be taken to power and you're certainly better off investing your time in other opportunities.

Prospects quite simply are not going to take action and spend good money on the things which are "on the list" but way down the page.

Getting access to power

Many sellers hesitate to ask for access to senior decision-makers because they fear offending their champion or creating resistance. But top sellers know that deals stall when the right people aren't involved.

The key is to position the request as a logical next step rather than making it seem like a power move. If the prospect resists, dig deeper to uncover what's really holding them back.

Below is an example from one of my discovery calls. The example shows how I look to gain access to power, without pushing too hard. What actually happens is I uncover unspoken concerns which are critical for me to address in order to gain the prospect's trust.

Me: *"Mary, from our conversation today, it feels like we've established we can help you. You've also mentioned in this* call that from all of the companies you've spoken to thus far, MySalesCoach is your preferred option. Is that fair?"

Mary: *"Yes, I'd say that's fair."*

Me: *"It sounds like for this to go anywhere, however, it would need to have buy-in from Sean. Would it be a bad idea to have him involved in our next conversation?"*

Mary: *"This will definitely need Sean's buy-in, but I'm not sure it's the right time to bring him in."*

Me: *"Reading between the lines, it feels like I haven't done a good enough job of earning your personal buy-in for you to feel confident taking me to Sean yet?"*

Mary: *"Now you raise it, there are definitely some things I still feel unsure about in regards to your coaches' credibility. The last call didn't really give me all the answers, and this is a really critical piece for us."*

Me: *"OK, no worries. I appreciate you wanting to be fully confident before taking us elsewhere. Shall we set some time up to go through the coach credibility piece in more detail?"*

Why This Works:

Secure Verbal Buy-In First

"You've also mentioned in this call that from all of the companies you've spoken to thus far, MySalesCoach is your preferred option. Is that fair?"

- Before pushing for access to power, I confirm that we are their preferred vendor.
- If they aren't leaning toward us, asking for access to senior stakeholders is premature and likely to be rejected.

Frame Power as a Logical Next Step

"It sounds like for this to go anywhere, it would need Sean's buy-in."

- Instead of saying *"I feel like I need to speak with Sean,"* which could create resistance, I get Mary to validate that Sean's involvement is necessary.

Use Reverse Psychology to Reduce Resistance

"Would it be a bad idea to have him involved in our next conversation?"

- Phrasing it this way forces Mary to argue against her own resistance.
- People are more likely to agree with something when it's framed as avoiding a mistake.

Call Out the Elephant in the Room

"Reading between the lines, it feels like I haven't done a good enough job of earning your own personal buy-in yet for you to feel confident taking me to Sean."

- Instead of pushing harder, I pause and reflect the resistance back onto myself.

- This reduces defensiveness while uncovering the real issue-Mary isn't fully on board yet and has legitimate concerns.

Keep the Deal Moving Forward

"Shall we set some time up to go through our coach's credibility in more detail?"

- Instead of forcing a conversation with Sean too early, I focus on addressing Mary's concerns first.
- This builds trust and sets up a stronger conversation later, when we do bring in power.

Sellers often assume that if a prospect resists bringing in power, they're being difficult or controlling. But in reality, they're usually just unsure about something themselves.

Instead of pushing past the resistance, address the hesitation head-on, because the real problem usually isn't access to power, it's that your champion isn't ready to take you there yet.

De-risking deal blockers

Many deals die in the final stages because a critical decision-maker gets involved too late and throws up roadblocks.

A smart seller pre-empts this by bringing power in early - but instead of forcing the issue, they frame it as a way to protect the prospect's time.

Below is an example from one of my calls, where I am trying to de-risk the deal being blocked, by getting my champion to involve power in the deal:

Me: *"So at this stage, what needs to happen internally for this to move forward?"*

Prospect: *"Well Rich, I need to finalise our internal business case and then bring it to our CRO."*

Me: *"Got it. And when similar investments have been made in the past, what's the biggest reason they've been approved... or blocked?"*

Prospect: *"Usually, it comes down to budget justification and making sure it aligns with broader company priorities."*

Me: *"That makes sense. I'd hate for you to spend time building out a business case, only for your CRO to push back because this didn't align with their priorities. Would it make sense to have a quick conversation with them now, just to get their initial thoughts and ensure we're on the right track?"*

Why This Works:

- This frames access to power as a way to protect their time.
- This implies risk - not bringing in power early could mean wasted effort.
- It positions the meeting as a "quick conversation" rather than a big ask.

Most prospects don't want to spend weeks working on something that gets rejected later. This framing makes it more likely that they proactively introduce you to power now, rather than later.

Understanding who the key stakeholders are

The average number of stakeholders involved in making a B2B buying decision sits at around 7-11 individuals. That number can vary depending on which source you look at and the size of the organisation you are selling to. What is indisputable however, is that there are more people involved in a decision than ever before, and that number isn't decreasing.

The book *The Jolt Effect* emphasises the fact that the key reason for deals dying is not due to companies preferring the status quo. It's due to prospects being nervous of making a bad decision. How do prospects protect themselves against making bad decisions? They shoulder the weight of the decision across many pairs of shoulders. If you aren't able to build trust and consensus with numerous stakeholders in your deal, then, quite frankly, you are increasing the risk of decision paralysis.

Top performing sellers don't settle for maintaining their dialogue and discovery with one or two stakeholders. They proactively engage as many of the buying committee as possible.

Ineffective salespeople get stuck at one stakeholder in their deals. See Chapters 12 and 14 for some practical tips to help you multi-thread here.

Early in my sales career, I made the mistake of taking a prospect's first answer at face value when I asked, "Who is the decision-maker?" If they said, "Our CEO," I would think, "Great, now I just need to get in front of the CEO and we're golden."

But as mentioned earlier, B2B deals simply don't get decided by just one person. Even if the CEO signs off, they don't make that decision in isolation. They lean on others for input, and those people can either build momentum for your deal or kill it before it ever reaches the CEO's desk.

That's why the better question isn't *"Who is the decision-maker?"* but rather, *"Who else cares about solving this problem?"*

The difference?

- The first question gives you a single point of contact, which is risky.
- The second question maps out the full buying committee, giving you multiple paths down which to push the deal forward.

Let's look at an example of how a simple shift in questioning reveals the real decision-making process.

Transcript 1: The First Answer (CEO as the Decision Maker)

Me: *"Who is key to this decision?"*

Prospect: *"Our CEO."*

Me: *"Got it; so your CEO would have final sign-off?"*

Prospect: *"Yeah, ultimately, they approve all major purchases."*

Me: *"That makes sense. And have they been involved in similar decisions like this before, or is this something they'd rely on others in the business to help guide?"*

Prospect: *"Well, they'd definitely take input from other people, but they'd be the final sign off."*

At this stage, I have confirmation that the CEO signs off (and is thus probably the power), but I don't yet know who actually influences the deal. I need to dig deeper.

Transcript 2: Understanding wider stakeholders

Me: *"Aside from sign-off, who else cares about tackling the problem surrounding the drop in conversion rates in your team's deals?"*

Prospect: *"Hmm... definitely our Head of Enablement, because they're responsible for training and making sure the team is executing well."*

Me: *"That makes total sense. And who else?"*

Prospect: *"Our two regional Sales Managers for sure. They're the ones responsible for the sales reps running these deals."*

Me: *"Got it. And typically when it comes to critical issues like conversion rates in deals, I tend to find the CRO has a big voice. Is that the case here too?"*

Prospect: *"Oh, 100%. They're always looking at revenue numbers and trying to figure out where we're losing deals."*

Me: *"That makes sense. And outside of the revenue team, does this issue impact anyone else?"*

Prospect: *"Potentially our HR Leader. They usually have oversight on anything to do with training, and may even be the budget holder for this kind of initiative. I'm not 100% sure though."*

Key Takeaways from This Approach:

1. The first answer ("CEO") was just the starting point. If I had stopped there, I would have focused only on final sign-off and ignored the influencers who actually shape the decision.
2. By broadening the question from "decision-makers" to "who else cares," I uncovered multiple key stakeholders. This naturally led the prospect to name the Head of Enablement, Sales Managers, CRO, and even HR as a potential budget holder.
3. Each follow-up question strategically expanded the buying committee. Asking *"who else?"* and referencing common decision influencers (e.g. the CRO) guided the prospect to think through the full picture.

4. The HR Leader was uncovered as a possible budget holder - something the prospect wasn't initially sure about. This is a crucial insight, as sellers often assume the budget sits with one person when, in reality, it may come from a different function.
5. This mapped out multiple paths for advancing the deal. Instead of relying on one person (who could delay or block the deal), I now knew that I needed to engage the Head of Enablement (execution), Sales Managers (day-to-day impact), CRO (high-level sponsor), and HR (potential budget holder).

Most sellers stop at the first answer and miss the bigger picture. By digging deeper, I now had multiple champions, influencers, and potential blockers mapped out, giving me a much stronger strategy to multi-thread and build momentum.

The CFO Test

In an ideal world, you'd always get a direct conversation with the CFO or whoever has final sign-off. But in reality? That doesn't always happen.

- Sometimes it's not necessary - if your champion is strong and has internal credibility, they can carry the deal forward.
- Sometimes it's impossible - senior stakeholders are protective of their time and won't take a meeting with a vendor unless their team has already sold them on the value.
- Sometimes your champion won't let you in - not

because they don't believe in the solution, but because they feel they need to sell it first before bringing you in.

So, if you can't be in the room, you need to know exactly how your champion is going to sell your solution behind closed doors. The way they frame the problem, handle objections, and justify the cost will determine whether your deal moves forward or dies.

You won't always get access to the CFO, but that doesn't mean you can't influence them. Your champion needs to sell this internally. If they go in with a weak pitch, your deal is dead. The best sellers don't just pitch to their champion; they coach them on how to pitch to power.

Below is a real example taken from one of my later stage discovery calls on an opportunity which involved MySalesCoach delivering an entire 12-month coaching programme to an SDR team. This was in month three of the sales cycle, and I had had several calls with different stakeholders in the deal. I had just finished co-building a business case with my champion:

Me: *"So once we finalise everything here, you'll be bringing this to your CFO, right?"*

Prospect: *"Yep."*

Me: *"Great. When you take this to them, what will you say is the key reason the business should invest in this?"*

Prospect: *"Well, I'm going to say this will really be the* *backbone of our Global SDR coaching strategy for 2025. SDR managers are super stretched and this is going to really supplement what they are doing"*

(Red Flag -"SDR managers are super stretched" is not a CFO-level reason to buy. In effect, this is simply a surface level issue.)

Me: *"Can I be direct? From experience, if you go to your CFO and say, 'Our SDR Managers are super stretched,' my concern is that she will push back and tell you to find ways to free up SDR Manager capacity. Do you share that concern?"*

Prospect: *"...Yeah, I see what you mean."*

Me: *"So let's go back to the business case that we discussed on our initial call. You mentioned that there's a 25% pipeline gap to close by the SDR team for the business to hit its revenue goals this year, and that unless they build an outbound mindset and skill set - this gap is unlikely to close. Is that still the case?*

Prospect: *"Yes... that's still definitely the case. Feels a bit more compelling doesn't it?!"*

(Now we're speaking in CFO language - hard numbers tied to revenue impact.)

Me: *"Perfect. Now, what do you think your CFO is going to push back on?"*

Prospect: *"Probably budget. Every additional spend request is being scrutinised right now."*

Me: *"And if they ask that, what will you say?"*

Prospect: *"...I'll tell them that this is a critical initiative that we simply can't deliver internally. There's some additional headcount that I was planning on making that I'm happy to hit pause on, if it means we funnel the spend to this instead"*

Key Takeaways:

Your Champion's First Pitch is Usually Too Weak

- If they pitch on "efficiency" or "managers are stretched," the CFO will push back.
- CFOs care about revenue, cost savings, or risk reduction - rarely anything else.

Reframe the Business Case in CFO Terms

- Challenge weak reasoning: "Would your CFO actually approve based on that?"
- Tie it to hard numbers: "You said there's a 25% pipeline gap - how does this solve that?"

Anticipate and Pressure-Test CFO Pushback

- Ask: "What's the first thing your CFO will push back on?"
- If they haven't thought about objections, they will crumble when questioned.

Make Budget a Trade-Off, Not an Obstacle

- If your champion is willing to cut something else to fund your solution, the deal is far more likely to get approved.

Most deals don't get lost because the CFO says no. They get lost because the champion makes a weak pitch and gets shut down.

If you can't be in the room, you need to know exactly what your champion will say when you're not there.

Want to make sure your deal doesn't die at the final hurdle? Before your champion speaks to power, ask:

- How will they sell your product/service in their own words?
- What's the #1 thing they will get push back on?
- How will they fight for this deal if they get push back?

If they can't answer confidently, your deal isn't ready. Get them ready before it's too late.

The best sellers don't just win over one person - they build internal momentum across an entire buying committee. If you aren't engaging multiple stakeholders, stress-testing your champion's pitch, and navigating power dynamics, you're rolling the dice. The question isn't *"Who is the decision-maker?"* It's *"How do I get buy-in across the buyer committee?"*

Slowing Down to Speed Up

One of the key things I've learned in sales is that sometimes, to speed a deal up, you have to slow it down.

Early in my career, I was obsessed with getting past my champion as quickly as possible to reach the "decision maker." I assumed that the faster I could get in front of the person who signed the contract, the better my chances of closing the deal were.

But that approach often backfired. I learned this the hard way in a coaching session, reviewing a deal I had lost because I was too eager to push forward.

I had a prospect - let's call her Rachel - who was a perfect fit for my solution. She ran a contact center, spent hours manually reviewing calls for QA, and knew her team was missing key upsell opportunities. She admitted that her current process was slow, inefficient, and reactive.

These were clear signs that my product could be of huge value to her.

But instead of fully engaging Rachel, getting her fully bought into how much better her world would be with my solution, I rushed to get in front of her MD. Rachel warned me that he wasn't ready for this conversation, but I pushed anyway. The result? She disengaged. I never heard from her again.

I lost the deal, not because the MD rejected me, but because I didn't first slow down to make Rachel my champion.

If I had taken my time, ensuring Rachel was fully on board, she would have been selling on my behalf. By the time we spoke to the MD, it wouldn't have been about product features; it would have been about business impact, with Rachel leading the case for change.

This experience also taught me a critical lesson: When a prospect says they need to involve others, your instinct might be to rush to that next meeting. Instead, consider slowing things down.

Here's how you can frame this to your prospect:

"Before we involve others, let's make sure you're fully confident in how this can help. That way, when we bring them in, you'll already know exactly how to position it internally."

By doing this, you achieve two things:

1. You create a champion who is invested in your solution.
2. You ensure that, when power gets involved, your champion is leading the conversation, not just introducing you as another vendor.

What happens when you skip this step?

When you rush to get multiple people in a meeting without a true champion:

- You risk having a stakeholder shut the deal down before it's had a chance to build momentum.

- Your champion hasn't had time to develop conviction, meaning they won't advocate for you when you're not in the room.
- Power will be less engaged because they haven't yet felt the pain or urgency to act.

Demo vs. Business Case

A common mistake sellers make when they do get access to power is assuming they need to do a full demo. In reality, most senior decision-makers don't care about features - they care about business impact.

A former colleague once challenged me before a meeting with a CEO. He asked, *"Do you really think the CEO wants a demo?"* It made me rethink my approach. Instead of diving into functionality, I opened the call by saying:

"When I speak to executives at your level, they usually fall into two categories: Some want a full demo to really get under the hood of our product and understand why others in the business have been excited about it. Others just want to discuss the business case. Which are you?"

The CEO immediately responded, *"Thank God you asked. I don't have time for a demo - let's talk about the business case."*

This shift in approach changed how I sold at the executive level. Instead of assuming what power wants, I ask them directly. More often than not, they just want to understand the ROI.

In complex B2B sales, the idea of a single "decision maker" is misleading. Deals are rarely closed by just one person - it's about engaging an entire buying committee. The key to success is identifying and winning over the real influencers, particularly those with power - the ability to secure budgets, move timelines, and drive internal change.

Key Takeaways:

- **Power matters**: The person who signs the contract isn't always the one driving the decision. Engage those who can accelerate the deal.
- **Speeding up by slowing down:** Rushing to senior executives before developing a champion within the organisation can kill momentum. First, ensure your champion is fully bought in.
- **Champions make or break deals:** Before engaging with power, equip your champion with the knowledge and confidence to sell internally on your behalf.
- **Multi-threading is essential:** Instead of focusing on a single "decision maker," map out who else influences the deal and build consensus across the buying committee.
- **The CFO Test:** If you can't be in the room, ensure your champion is prepared to pitch the business case in terms that resonate with senior leadership.
- **Tailor executive conversations:** Many executives don't want a feature-heavy demo; they care

about business impact. Ask them directly what they value - most will prioritise ROI over product details.

By strategically navigating access to power, securing internal champions, and aligning with the broader buying committee, you can reduce deal risk, shorten sales cycles, and increase win rates.

Chapter Eleven

Pricing and Negotiation

Selling vs. Negotiating: Knowing the Difference

One of the biggest mistakes sales reps make is treating selling and negotiating as the same thing. They're not.

Selling is helping the prospect see the value of your solution and aligning it to their needs.

Negotiating happens when the prospect sees the value but wants to tweak the terms - price, contract length, payment terms, implementation, or scope.

If you find yourself negotiating before the prospect fully understands the value of what you provide, you're not negotiating - you're still selling. And if you move to pricing discussions too soon, you'll find yourself negotiating from a position of weakness.

A good rule of thumb: You shouldn't negotiate until the prospect wants what you have.

This is why strong discovery is your greatest weapon in negotiation. If the prospect hasn't articulated the pain they're trying to solve, the cost of inaction, and the impact of solving it, they'll see your pricing as an expense rather than an investment.

Conclusion: Great selling leads to less negotiation.

Ironically, a lot of things that have been covered in the book so far reinforce the idea that when great discovery is done - when a prospect's world is truly understood, when their problem and the size of that problem is clear, and when the cost of inaction is made explicit - negotiation becomes less of an issue. When the pain of doing nothing is fully realised, people will feel less inclined to push back on price or negotiate aggressively.

I think many salespeople feel like negotiation is something that all buyers will do in every deal. Actually, I've experienced many deals in my career where there was no negotiation. The prospect felt the terms of the deal were ultimately fair, and they were so keen to solve the problem that the order form was signed without any question.

Recently, I saw a sales trainer on LinkedIn say that for every deal they run, they come to the "negotiation call" with a "discount". The implication is that a discount is simply part of their process. This is madness for me. Not only is it madness that a sales trainer is advocating for discounts as standard, it makes the assumption that every prospect will expect one. It shows a huge lack of belief in the product or service you are selling.

But the truth is, negotiation is something we will all experience from time to time in our deals. The key is having the right strategy, understanding the mind of the buyer, and being aware of killer mistakes (many of which we have committed in our career).

To start with, let's get a deeper appreciation of the reasons prospects want to negotiate with us.

Why Do People Negotiate?

Understanding why buyers negotiate in the first place is crucial. They don't always do it because they actually need a better price. Often, negotiation is about perception and psychology as much as it is about cost.

1. **To Look Good to Their Boss** - Buyers want to feel like they've done a great job, and that they have secured the best possible deal for their company. They want recognition for achieving cost savings, even on something they were going to buy anyway. This is something that can be deeply ingrained in buying behaviour. I know all this, as I have done this many times myself as a buyer in the past!

2. **For the Feeling of a Good Deal** - The thrill of getting a bargain is powerful. People love the sense that they have saved money, even when they didn't need to. A personal example: recently, I bought a new pair of trainers, not because I needed them, but because they were discounted. The justification? They were originally priced at £150 but I paid £80. That feeling of getting a deal drove the purchase. Moreover, I felt it gave me a good justification for my wife as to why I had bought a pair of trainers I probably didn't truly need.

3. **Budget Constraints** - Some buyers genuinely do have a set amount of money to work with. The budget isn't flexible, and they must operate within that limit. In some cases, finding additional funds simply isn't an option. When I went to buy a new car, I simply did not have the money to buy the new model. I could only afford the older model. These were the cold hard facts that the car salesman didn't seem to understand.

4. **Cash Flow Issues** - Sometimes, it's not the total cost that concerns a buyer, but how and when they have to pay. Companies with cash flow constraints may not mind the price itself, but the payment terms - whether they can spread costs over time-become a major factor in negotiations.

5. **Not Seeing Full Value** - If a buyer doesn't fully understand the value of a solution, they will naturally try to negotiate. They may see partial value but not enough to justify the full price. In these cases, the real problem isn't price; it's an incomplete understanding of the ROI.

6. **To Reduce Risk** - Buyers can be cautious. Companies are always looking to de-risk, particularly in times of economic turbulence. Some buyers want to negotiate on things like term length, to protect themselves if things go wrong, or if the product doesn't deliver as expected. Sometimes, this comes from a past experience of "being burnt".

7. **Tactical Negotiation** - Some buyers have already decided to go with a competitor but will still engage in negotiations. Their goal is to get a lower price to take back to the preferred vendor and force them to match or beat the offer.

Part of the challenge of negotiation is to get an understanding of which of the above (non-exhaustive) reasons is the explanation for why somebody is negotiating in the first place. If you spend time trying to understand this, then you are automatically going to be in a stronger position of negotiating influence.

The Psychology of Money

One of the main reasons salespeople struggle with negotiation is the intrinsic discomfort they have talking about money full stop. In fact, Objective Management Group, who have assessed over 2.5 million salespeople, identified that 43% of all sellers are uncomfortable talking about money. This leads to the following:

Avoiding the Money Conversation - Salespeople either gloss over budget discussions, avoid asking about money altogether, or ignore budget constraints when they arise.

Lack of Pricing Intelligence - They fail to understand competitor pricing and don't confirm whether the prospect has the budget or willingness to spend before providing a quote.

Inability to Sell Value - Without knowing the budget or competitive landscape, they struggle to position their pricing in context, leading to price objections.

Longer and Riskier Sales Cycles - By skipping key money conversations, they increase back-and-forth negotiations, and risk stalling deals, or even losing them without a chance to review pricing.

So where does this discomfort come from?

It's not just about tactics: it's about deep-rooted beliefs formed from childhood.

Cultural Conditioning from Childhood

- Think back to when you were a kid. You never knew how much your parents earned. Money was a private matter, never openly discussed.
- You probably heard phrases like "Everything is expensive in life." And as adults, we can relate to this: it *is* expensive!
- But this mindset carries into adulthood, making money conversations feel uncomfortable, even in professional settings.

Money as a Taboo Subject

- Many of us grow up believing that talking about money is off limits - so much so that even in job interviews, salespeople struggle to negotiate their own salaries!

- Collectively we have interviewed well over 100 salespeople and could count on one hand the number who tried to negotiate their pay. This is ironic - if you can't confidently negotiate your salary, how can you confidently negotiate deals?

The Personal Attachment to Money

- People subconsciously attach personal meaning to money, viewing it through their own experiences.
- I recall once in the very early part of my career, pricing a deal at £20,000, while my own salary was only £17,000 per year. It felt ludicrous to me that a company would pay more for my product than I made in a year - but that was my mental barrier, not theirs. To the company, £20,000 was nothing. I was just anchored to my own financial perspective.

What seems like a big number to you might be pocket change to your buyer. When salespeople detach from personal financial experiences and step into the prospect's world, they negotiate with more confidence, clarity, and control.

Win-Win vs. Win-Lose Negotiation

There are two fundamental negotiation models: win-win and win-lose. The win-win model seeks to create a mutually beneficial outcome. These conversations tend to be cooperative, and the result is a happy, long-term relationship. Conversely, the win-lose model is adversarial, where one side feels like they have been defeated. The losing party often seeks retribution, whether consciously or unconsciously.

When a buyer walks away feeling like they didn't get a fair deal, they will nitpick every aspect of the relationship, looking for faults. If a seller feels they lost in the negotiation, they might not prioritise the customer's success. I recall a deal where I was negotiated down so aggressively by the prospect that, by the end, I was left with a bitter feeling toward the customer. In fact, I'd practically lost interest in the deal. As a result, there was little interest in ensuring their ongoing success. This negative dynamic can strain relationships for years, not to mention the fact that you can hamstring yourself on pricing or terms for long periods of time.

Quite simply - if one party feels like they lost a negotiation, it rarely pans out well in the long run.

The Seven Deadly Sins of Negotiation

1. **Failure to Sell Well** - When discovery is weak, negotiation becomes difficult. If the prospect doesn't clearly see the value of the solution, they will push harder on price.
2. **Negotiating Against Yourself** - Salespeople often lower their price or offer concessions before the buyer even asks for them. Using words like "typically" or "usually" invites prospects to push for alternative terms.
3. **Negotiating Too Soon** - Never negotiate before knowing you are the preferred vendor. Asking, *"If*

211

price wasn't an issue, how comfortable would you be moving forward?" ensures commitment before engaging in pricing discussions.

4. **Thinking Money is Always the Issue** - Price is rarely the only obstacle. Other factors such as stakeholder alignment, implementation, and risk mitigation often hold equal or greater weight.

5. **Death by 1,000 Cuts** - When a buyer keeps making incremental requests (e.g., lower price, removing auto-renewal, smaller commitments), the deal becomes eroded piece by piece. Instead, gather all requests upfront and negotiate holistically.

6. **Not Involving Your Champion** - If a champion isn't present in negotiations, the conversation revolves around cost rather than value. Ensuring that internal advocates participate strengthens the case for your solution.

7. **Not Seeing Negotiation as a Trade-Off** - Every concession should come with a return. If a discount is requested, ask for a longer contract term, additional licenses, or a case study.

Sources of Leverage in Negotiation

Negotiation isn't just about being smart with discounts. It's about leverage. There are multiple sources of leverage that can shift the balance of power in a negotiation:

1. **Beliefs** - Confidence in the product, company, and personal ability makes a huge difference. Perhaps some of you have worked at companies

where you didn't truly believe in the value of your product or service. If the product being sold doesn't feel particularly valuable to the seller, it becomes difficult to defend the price. Conversely, when you are selling something you truly believe in that you know delivers exceptional value to your customers, then this will shine through in how you sell it. It usually means that you will stand by its value in negotiations, and will be less inclined to do a "race to the bottom" to win the customer's business.

2. **Needs and Understanding** - The deeper your understanding of a prospect's pain is, the easier it is to negotiate. If they are experiencing acute pain, they won't just spend money to fix it - they'll do so quickly and with fewer objections. I was selling to a VP Global Sales late last year. They told me that they had a 25% pipeline gap they needed to close by Q3 of this year. His neck was on the line in solving this problem, so he needed to make a change quickly to give him enough time to fix the problem. The negotiation was quick and light touch. He didn't want to waste time negotiating over every aspect of the deal, as it was time being wasted on fixing the business problem.

3. **Emotion** - People make emotional decisions in negotiation. Some get frustrated, angry, or desperate. Staying calm and measured ensures a better outcome. I remember watching one of my sales reps getting irate with a prospect who was

negotiating with them. It started to make them develop an adversarial mindset, which ran the risk of the whole relationship breaking down. When you stay calm and measured, you come across as more reasoned to the buyer. When the buyer sees you as reasoned, then they are going to be more willing to have a fair outcome for both parties.

4. **Power Relationships** - Getting to the right decision-makers is crucial. Lower-level employees often negotiate harder to prove themselves, while executives focus on solving business problems quickly. Low-level buyers feel like they can boost their reputation by getting a good deal. Senior executives who are trying to solve big business problems worth significantly more than a small discount, care less about being seen as good negotiators than being seen as people who drive business strategy.

5. **Pipeline Strength** - The stronger the pipeline, the stronger the negotiation position. When there are plenty of deals in play, there is no desperation to close a particular one, allowing the seller to hold firm on terms. Some of my best negotiation has been done when I knew I had plenty of deals close to closing. Equally, when I've been going through a rough patch, my negotiation perhaps sounded desperate (and rarely worked).

Tough Negotiation Stories from Real Deals

Lesson 1: The Cost of Desperation

In the early days of Refract, there was a rough patch where no deals had been closed for weeks. There was a well-developed deal in the pipeline, but the prospect showed no urgency. In an effort to close the deal quickly, a desperate discount was offered. The prospect didn't immediately take the discount, but a month later they did - after it was no longer helpful to that quarter's numbers. Too much had been given away for nothing in return, and the experience was deeply frustrating. Never negotiate from a position of desperation, and always ensure urgency aligns with your sales cycle.

Lesson 2: The Danger of Death by 1,000 Cuts

I was involved in a deal with a Mid-Market tech company where the prospect kept making incremental requests after sending the contract: first, a cheaper price, then a request to remove an auto-renewal clause, then fewer user licenses, then switching to a quarterly rolling contract. Each time the order form was updated and sent over, another request came back. Each time I felt it would be the last one. But they kept coming. This is the classic "death by 1,000 cuts." When your prospect keeps making requests one after another, as a seller, you get to the point of no return, and simply accept their demands to get the deal done.

Lesson 3: Why You Should Never Discount Too Soon

A seller once quoted £20,000 for a solution. The prospect responded, "That's a lot more than I was expecting." Instead of probing further, the seller immediately asked, "What if we looked at bringing the cost down?" This is the definition of negotiating against yourself.

Lesson 4: The Perils of Weak Language

I listened to a call once where the prospect asked about contract terms. The response? "Typically, we look to do annual agreements." That single word, "typically", invited negotiation. The prospect immediately knew that there were more flexible options they could leverage.

Pricing and Negotiation Lessons

Below are a series of real situations that have arisen from our own calls when it came to discussing pricing or negotiating on terms with the buyer. Hopefully these can be helpful in you having higher impact conversations with your own buyers in similar situations.

1. Handling the Early Request for Pricing

A common mistake many sales reps make is avoiding the pricing conversation early on, thinking they are thus maintaining control. However, this often leads to frustration for the prospect. I remember having the mindset of not giving a price until "the prospect sees the value". When I think of how I personally like to buy, if

I asked for a price and the salesperson refused to even give me an indication, it would really wind me up. So that was the ultimate in double standards! The best approach is to acknowledge the importance of pricing while maintaining control of the discussion.

Prospect: "Before we go on, can you give me an idea of how much this costs?"

Salesperson: *"I'm happy to go through pricing at a high level. Just so I understand, is pricing the main driver for you here?"*

By framing the conversation this way, you get valuable insights into how price-sensitive the prospect is. If price is the key issue, it's a sign that you may be dealing with a buyer who is shopping purely on cost.

2. Handling "Way Too Expensive" Reactions

When a prospect says, "That's far too expensive," they already have an expectation of what they think the price should be. Instead of panicking or discounting, dig deeper:

Salesperson: *"Help me understand - what were you expecting this to be?"*

This approach accomplishes two things:

1. It surfaces their price expectation, which may be based on incorrect assumptions.
2. It allows you to determine whether they are comparing you to a lower-quality alternative.

If they mention a much lower price, respond:

Salesperson: "I feel like we are quite far apart on expectations. Typically, when I hear that, it's because the buyer is comparing us to a cheaper alternative. Would you mind sharing what you're comparing us to?"

This ensures you are not discounting prematurely and allows you to reframe the conversation around value.

3. Handling Multi-Year Discounts the Right Way

Many sales reps offer blanket discounts on multi-year deals, which can create renewal problems later.

Imagine a salesperson is negotiating a £100,000 per year deal for a three-year contract. The prospect pushes for a 10% discount, and the salesperson agrees - but applies the discount to all three years instead of just Year 1.

What happened?

- If they discounted all three years:
    - ☐ £100,000 → £90,000 per year.
    - ☐ Total contract value: £270,000 instead of £300,000.
    - ☐ £30,000 lost over three years
- If they only discounted Year 1:
    - ☐ Year 1: £90,000.
    - ☐ Years 2 and 3: £100,000 each.
    - ☐ Total contract value: £290,000.
    - ☐ Only £10,000 lost.

. Instead, structure discounts strategically:

- Year 1: Discounted rate.
- Years 2 and 3: Price freeze (instead of additional discounts).

This ensures that, while the customer gets a lower entry point, they don't lock in an unsustainable discount structure that makes future pricing discussions difficult.

4. Responding When a Buyer Wants to Speak to a Customer

Prospects often ask, "Can I speak to a customer?" Sales reps dread this because it means asking for favours. Instead of treating it as a hurdle, use it as leverage:

Salesperson: "We do arrange customer calls, but only for prospects who are almost at the point of being ready to move forward and this is the last thing they need to get comfortable with. If we provide that introduction, would you be ready to proceed?"

This ensures that customer conversations are only happening at the right stage and helps avoid wasting valuable customer goodwill.

5. The Free Trial Mistake

A common mistake is offering a trial or POC by default, assuming it's necessary for the sale. Many founders and sales reps do this because they lack confidence in their product's value.

Instead of proactively offering a free trial, wait until the prospect asks, then position it as a negotiation lever:

Salesperson: "A free trial is something we offer selectively as it involves cost and effort for ourselves as well as for you. If we did provide one, would you be comfortable agreeing to some success metrics that, if we satisfied them, would see us moving forward?"

This ensures the trial is used strategically rather than being given away unnecessarily.

6. Pre-Agreed Referrals

Most sales reps hesitate to ask for referrals, even though referrals are one of the most powerful ways to generate new business. The best way to handle this is to make it part of the deal upfront.

Salesperson: "If we move forward, would you be open to providing a referral once you've seen the value in the first few months?"

By setting this expectation early, it becomes a natural part of the agreement rather than an awkward afterthought.

7. Confirming You're the Vendor of Choice

Salespeople often negotiate before they know they are the preferred partner of choice from the prospect. It's the equivalent of chucking discounts over a fence and hoping they somehow magically work.

A massive rule of thumb. NEVER negotiate until the prospect has confirmed you are their vendor of choice.

Prospect: "We really like the solution, but the pricing is a bit higher than we were expecting. Can you come down on price?"

Salesperson: "I appreciate you being upfront about that. Just so I understand, aside from pricing, is there anything else stopping you from moving forward with us?"

(This question flushes out any hidden objections before discussing price.)

Prospect: "No, it's just the price at this point."

Salesperson: "Got it. That's helpful to know. Just to confirm, I know you have been evaluating a number of options; is it fair to assume therefore that we are your preferred partner here?"

(This ensures that the negotiation isn't premature - if they're still evaluating other options, discounting may be pointless.)

Prospect: "Yes, we want to move forward with you, but we need to get the cost down by £2,000 to get this into a budget line, which means we don't need to seek further approval."

Salesperson: "That makes sense. If we were able to be flexible on pricing, would you be comfortable moving forward today?"

(This creates urgency and ensures the discount isn't just being used to leverage against competitors.)

Prospect: "We'd be ready to sign if we can agree on the pricing."

Salesperson: "Okay, let me see what I can do. If we were able to offer some flexibility, would you be open to committing to a multi-year agreement or providing a case study down the line?"

(This reframes the negotiation into a win-win exchange rather than a simple price cut.)

Prospect: "We could do a two-year agreement, potentially."

Salesperson: "That's really helpful. Let me take this back internally and see what's possible."

(Now, the salesperson has positioned themselves to negotiate from strength, ensuring they're not discounting for the sake of it, but in exchange for commitment.)

8. Giving things away that aren't price

Too many salespeople think that price is the only thing the prospect wants you to concede on when it comes to negotiation. The story below shows a case where the cost of the deal was not the real issue, and I was able to hold the full value of the deal, but made the prospect comfortable with the outcome:

Prospect: "I'm keen to move forward, but now isn't the right time to pull the trigger"

Salesperson: "OK. Can you help me understand what's holding you back?"

Prospect: "I can't sign up to this before our new budgetary cycle kicks in in two months' time. It's really an accounting issue. So maybe we should talk in two months' time."

Salesperson: "I totally hear you. I'm not sure if this will work for you, but I have a suggestion. It's clear we can start to help your team right now. Would you be open to signing an agreement now, but we don't invoice you for two months? In the meantime, I can give your team access to our group sessions, ultimately free of charge."

Prospect: "That's a great idea actually. I'm pretty sure I can swing that"

This negotiation effectively uncovers the real objection (budget cycle timing) rather than accepting a delay at face value. I offer a creative, low-risk solution: sign now, defer invoicing, and provide immediate value. This turned a potential stall into a win-win commitment.

Summary: Negotiation is About Control, Not Concessions

Negotiation isn't about lowering prices; it's about ensuring both sides feel like they're getting a fair deal. If you've done great discovery, built value, and negotiated strategically, pricing shouldn't feel like an obstacle.

- Separate selling from negotiating. Don't negotiate before they see the value.
- Understand why people negotiate. Not every objection is about price.
- Avoid the seven deadly sins. Don't negotiate over email, discount too soon, or cave quickly.
- Use the "give-to-get" rule. This means you always trade concessions.
- Project confidence. The way you say the price matters.
- Know when to walk away. Not every deal is worth closing.

The best negotiators aren't the ones who discount the most. They're the ones who make the prospect feel like they got a great deal, while keeping the value intact.

Chapter Twelve

Post-Discovery

Most salespeople really seem to struggle with what to do when their discovery call comes to an end. They book in a next step one or two weeks out with the prospect, and they sit there waiting for time to pass before they can have that next valuable conversation, hoping that the prospect will deliver some great news.

Is it any wonder that so many prospects cancel or push out that next call? Their schedules fill up, their mind gets focused on other tasks, and that next conversation with you looks like the easiest meeting in the world to push out.

As we say, time kills deals; in a world full of even more distractions, economic turbulence, and competition, just sitting on your hands and awaiting your next call is not a good strategy.

What you do next, after your discovery call, is nearly as crucial as what you do in the call itself.

Replay the call

One of the things I realised soon after launching Refract (a conversation intelligence platform) to the market, was the huge benefit of self-reflection. I found I gained so much value from replaying my sales call recordings: even immediately after I had come off the call.

Here is what I learned from doing this:

- There were a number of things the prospect had shared with me on the call which I simply hadn't picked up on during the call itself. In some cases, these included really crucial details about their situation which could materially change the direction, or speed of a deal. I realised that my active listening skills weren't as strong as I had thought. I remember one call where, listening back to the call, the prospect revealed a competitor they were already using. Alarmingly I just hadn't heard it the first time round. From listening to hundreds of discovery calls over the past few years, this is a problem which is universal across all sellers. Critical details, nuances, and pieces of information are simply not heard by sellers when they are in the heat of a discovery call; that is why listening back is so important to do. I challenge anybody to do this and I *guarantee* you will identify things second time round which you didn't pick up on the first time round.

- Listening back gave me fuel to dive deeper into certain topics with the prospect in our next conversation or even to try and figure them out between scheduled calls. I could say to prospects things like: "one thing you mentioned in our last call which I feel I didn't completely understand was about the skill gaps in your sales team. Could you tell me more about that?" Some people may feel scared about sounding stupid to their prospects by doing this. In fact the opposite is true. They end up sounding curious, eager to understand, and, above all, like someone trying to help the prospect rather than just selling to them.

- These reviews gave me my "demo menu'". I was able to digest the three or four specific pain points being faced by the prospect that I believed I could solve, and it enabled me to create my WIHYS (What I Heard You Say) slide. This slide would essentially provide my agenda for my demo and enable me to deliver a tailored demonstration which specifically nailed each of the prospect's pain points. I'll return to this later in this chapter.

On top of this, listening back to your discovery calls is simply just good practice in enabling you to figure out how to get better at the process. Which questions worked? Which didn't? What did you regret not asking? Where did you monologue for too long? What objections did you face that you didn't handle well? Where in the call do you need some coaching?

Some people may see this as a chore. In my eyes, it's a high-stakes activity that all sellers should be doing.

Post-Discovery Call Email

I remember what I used to do at the end of my discovery call. Next to nothing.

I would send a generic invite for the next call, and, if I could be bothered, I would send a half-baked email to the prospect that looked something like this:

Thanks!   _ ⤢ ✕

john.doe@acme.com

Thanks!|

John

Thanks for your time just now. I've sent an invite for our next call which is next Tuesday.

Look forward to speaking then!

Rich

Looking back now, this just appeared lazy, unthoughtful, and lacking in any sort of value. Quite frankly, I might as well not have sent one at all!

After your discovery call, you have a real chance to make a second great impression on your prospect. This is why investing a little bit of time and attention to your post-discovery call follow-up is a no brainer.

Here is the method I have since started using, and it's free for you to steal too:

1. Here is my understanding.
2. Problems you have shared.
3. Why are you looking to solve these problems?
4. What's going to happen next?
5. Additional value.

You can see this method in play below:

Notice that the email is highly specific, and focused on the prospect's situation and the specific challenges they are facing. What do you think is going through the prospect's mind when they are reading this? They undoubtedly feel like they have been listened to by the seller, as well as feeling they have a genuine reason to show up to the next call.

Steve

Good to connect earlier. Here is my understanding of the situation. Did I get this down correctly?

- You have a team of 20 AE's in UK with a vision to grow in the next 12 months

- Sales cycles have started getting longer of late

- Your conversion ratios have dropped by about 15% since this time last year

- Need to train your reps on a more effective means of doing discovery.

- Need to fix this by EOY as the company is looking to raise their Series B and need to prove success to investors

- A win for you personally could mean getting a global role

Sent an invite to yourself and your CRO for a meeting next Thursday at 2:00pm, where I will walk you through my training content to see if it fits.

In the meantime, here's a resource I put together with some quick tips on discovery which should help in the meantime.

Rich

Notice there is no "selling" of my product or service. It is all completely focused on the prospect's situation and the problems that have been identified in discovery. Obviously you can only construct emails like this if you have had good discovery...but that is why you need to have been paying attention to the previous chapters!

Finally, notice the "additional value" I'm giving at the end of the email. In this case, it's a resource centered on discovery tactics as that is the exact problem the prospect is facing. Think about the useful resources you may want to share with your prospects as a "give" after your discovery calls. Whether or not they look at them is not the point. It's the fact you are showing yourself as a trusted advisor and someone who stands out against the competition.

Using AI to Optimise Your Follow-Up Emails

I highly recommend leveraging generative AI tools such as ChatGPT, to speed up your follow-up process from discovery conversations. Here is a quick workflow and prompt you can use to help you here:

1. Prompt: I am going to upload an example template of an email I have sent to a prospect following on from my discovery call with them. Please use this template for creating future follow-up emails. Note that I am focusing on the prospect's situation and their sales challenges. Also note the general length of the email. To create the emails, I will drop in the call transcript from the call itself. Please remember that this template is called "disco follow-up".

2. Copy and paste in an example wrap-up email like the one above.

3. Copy and paste in the call transcript from your call recording tool of choice.

4. Copy and paste the summary email into your email service and make any tweaks accordingly.

What you'll find is that you're able to craft compelling follow-up emails in seconds, and they will really make a mark with prospects. You've also just bought yourself back plenty of time, which you can re-invest in a WIHYS slide (see next section), or other revenue-generating activities!

WIHYS Slide

Ahead of your next conversion with the prospect (which could be a demo), it is wise to prepare a "What I Heard You Say Slide".

The objective of this slide is to:

- Show the prospect at the start of your next conversation that you listened to them.
- Show the prospect you understood their situation accurately (and this allows prospects to course correct you if not).
- Give you the opportunity to do further discovery and/or clarify any areas. (Note that I am looking to clarify the pipeline shortfall in my example below).
- Help bring other stakeholders up to speed on the conversation.
- Provide a great framework through which to direct your demo/presentation, ensuring that you just talk about the prospect's key problems and challenges. In other words, this stops you from "showing up and throwing up".

Once you have created a template here, creating this slide should not take too long once you are in the practice of listening back to your calls. Believe me - it's well worth it. If nothing else, it gets you "back in the zone" of the deal and is great pre-call preparation.

WHAT I HEARD YOU SAY

- Sales Maturity:

-When John joined 6 months ago, the sales team was at 2-3/10 on a maturity scale. Now at 4-5/10, the goal is to reach 8/10 by year-end.

- Skill Gaps:

-Pipeline Generation: Improved since July but still inconsistent, with reps struggling to generate enough quality opportunities. This needs to change if John is to hit his 2025 goals. - **What is the shortfall here?**

-Increasing Deal Size: Historic pricing led to low-value deals. Reps need stronger consultative selling skills to drive higher ACVs. ACV needs to grow by 40% otherwise at risk of missing plan.

-Prospecting Confidence: Some reps lack confidence and strategy, creating inconsistent results.

-If John was to hit his plan this year, this will open up opportunities for more of a European role (currently just UK focused)

- Team Composition:

-10 current new business reps, growing to 14 by May (Mid-market, enterprise-focused).

-Reps are full-cycle, relying on self-generated pipeline due to immature marketing/demand gen functions.

-Leadership Gap: No experienced sales managers. John cannot dedicate the necessary coaching time (3+ hours per rep/month).

Multithreading post-discovery

As we've seen, the average number of stakeholders involved in a B2B buying decision has been sharply rising in recent years.

Post-discovery, you are missing a trick if you are not being proactive in building connections with the wider buying committee. Don't just sit there and wait for the person you have just spoken with to open doors. The more lines of contact you can open up, the more you start de-risking your deal (in case someone goes silent or even leaves the business), as well as making yourself more memorable and differentiated.

But how do you go about doing this in a way which feels meaningful, non-salesy, and in a way that makes your key contact not feel like you are stepping out of line?

Here are some ideas:

Asking for an intro

So your best opportunity to multi-thread is on the discovery call itself. But in order to get access to key stakeholders, timing and how you ask for those introductions is always key. Asking for introductions before you've built up enough trust with the prospect is likely to be met with resistance. So if you feel like you haven't got to at least Level 3 on the pyramid, don't be surprised when your prospect resists making other introductions. However, if you do feel like you've "earned the right", here's a talk track you can leverage:

"Frank, you mentioned earlier that Cassie is someone who would care about solving the problem around improving consultative selling skills. From experience, when key stakeholders like Cassie aren't involved in conversations, they can sometimes feel left out. Would you be open to connecting me to Cassie after this call? I'm happy to speak with her one-on-one to make sure it's relevant for her to invest more time in exploring this with us"

Emphasise the problem. Use emotion as a reason to involve others. Make them feel safe and not threatened.

LinkedIn Connection

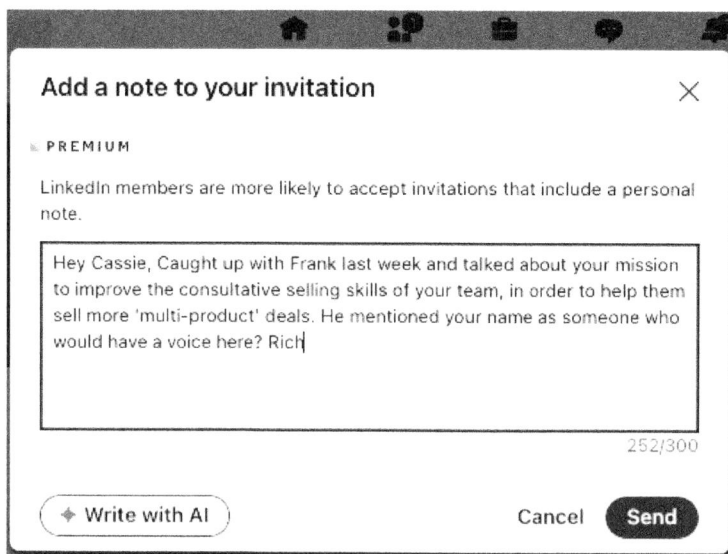

If your contact has mentioned the names of other relevant stakeholders, connect with them on LinkedIn and construct a message that reinforces the specific key challenge discussed, and will make the new contact pay attention. Don't unnecessarily push for a meeting though.

Send a video

Want to stand out while multi-threading? Send a video! It staggers me how few salespeople are using video as part of their sales engagement. Consider how much more you can stand out by sending a personal video to new stakeholders, rather than a bland email.

Here's a script for you to steal

> "Hey Cassie - hopefully you like getting videos like this!
>
> I just came off a call with Frank. We talked about some of your goals this year surrounding multi-product opportunities, and some of the challenges your reps are facing with selling higher ACV deals.
>
> We talked briefly about how MySalesCoach might be able to support this mission through 1:1 coaching. Frank said you have a big voice here, and so you may consider joining our next conversation next Thursday at 2:00pm.
>
> By the way, noticed you are connected to Nick over at ACME. We've just helped his team address this specific problem"

- Be concise and to the point.
- Reference conversations with someone they work with.
- Talk about the specific problem they will care about.
- Mention the option of them joining the next call, but don't push it.
- Reference social proof or something personal.

Key Takeaways

Most sellers think post-discovery is about waiting. Top sellers know it's about staying engaged.

- **Replay your calls** - You'll always catch something new.
- **Send strong follow-ups** - Don't let them forget why they booked the next meeting.
- **Prepare for the next conversation** - Your ability to effectively prepare for follow-up conversations can make all the difference in building trust with your buyer
- **Multi-thread early** - get more people involved before it's too late.

Sales happens between the meetings, not just during them. The question is: are you taking control of that time?

Chapter Thirteen

Additional Tips and Tricks

At this stage, you've got the fundamentals of a high-quality discovery call nailed. You know how to structure it, ask better questions, and keep control. But sales isn't just about the basics - it's about the fine margins.

This chapter is about the extra 1% - the techniques, mindset shifts, and tactical plays that separate the elite from the average. Get these right, and you'll convert more deals, faster, with less resistance.

The Doctor-Patient Mindset

One of the biggest mindset shifts elite sellers make is treating discovery like a doctor-patient relationship. This analogy isn't ours, (I believe it's Mark Roberge's), but we live by it.

Think about what happens when you visit a doctor.

- They've already reviewed your notes before you arrive. They know your medical history, your last visit, and any previous issues.
- They start with an open-ended question: "What brings you in today?"
- They don't rush to prescribe medication. Instead, they ask specific, investigative questions to ensure

they fully understand the problem before making a recommendation.

If you walked into a doctor's office with a chesty cough, they wouldn't immediately throw antibiotics at you. Instead, they'd run a full diagnosis:

- When did it start?
- How long have you had it?
- What colour is the mucus?
- Any other symptoms?
- What medication have you already tried?
- Any family history of this?

They piece together a full picture before making a recommendation.

And when they finally do hand over a prescription, do you say:

- "Can I think it over?"
- "Can I get a second opinion?"
- "Can I have a free trial?"

No. You trust them. You follow their recommendation without hesitation.

Why This Matters in Sales

Elite sellers operate the same way.

- They never rush to pitch solutions - they diagnose first.

- They ask tough questions without fear of offending - just like a doctor who asks personal, uncomfortable questions if need be.
- They qualify out when necessary - a doctor won't prescribe unnecessary medicine. If they think you'll be fine in two weeks, they'll tell you to go home. Salespeople should do the same.
- They will send you elsewhere if they need to - just like a doctor refers patients to specialists when necessary. If a prospect isn't a good fit, point them in the right direction.
- They don't rely on credentials to build trust - doctors don't talk about where they studied, how many patients they've helped, or how long they've been practicing. You trust them because of the way they run the interaction.

The Bottom Line

Most people don't even know their doctor's first name - yet they trust them implicitly.

Why? Because the doctor made them feel understood and prescribed the right solution.

When a discovery call ends, your prospect should feel the same way.

Mirroring - a Subtle Power Move

Mirroring is one of the simplest yet most powerful techniques in sales. It's a low-effort, high-impact way to get prospects to open up, expand on their thoughts, and reveal more than they originally intended, without feeling like they're being grilled.

Here's how it works: you repeat back the last few words of their sentence, slightly raising your tone so it feels like a natural question.

At first, it might feel too basic to be useful, but when it is done right, mirroring can completely change the depth of your discovery calls. It helps you slow the conversation down, get clearer answers, and, most importantly, stop making assumptions.

Why Mirroring Works So Well

1. **Prospects keep talking:** People naturally expand when they hear their own words repeated back to them. It makes them feel heard and subtly encourages them to explain further.

2. **It forces clarity:** Prospects often give vague answers that don't tell you much (*"Our pipeline isn't great right now."*). Mirroring nudges them to be more specific, so you don't waste time guessing what they mean.

3. **It slows things down:** Sales reps are usually too eager to move from one question to the next, but the best conversations happen in the gaps. Mirroring forces you to be present and let the prospect fill in the blanks.

4. **It makes you sound like you're actually listening:** Because, well… you are. And when a prospect feels listened to, they're far more likely to trust you

I'll bring this to life with some examples from my discovery calls

Expanding on a Vague Statement

Prospect: *"Our results haven't been great recently."*

Me: *"Recently?"*

Prospect: *"Yeah, the last two quarters have been rough. The pipeline is down, and the team isn't closing enough."*

Boom. With one word, we've just unlocked the real problem - pipeline and close rates, all without asking a single direct question. If I'd just nodded along and moved on, I'd be operating on surface-level information.

Digging into a Hidden Concern

Prospect: *"We're not too concerned about churn rates right now."*

Me: *"Right now?"*

Prospect: *"Well... actually, we do have concerns about future churn once contract cycles come up for renewal."*

See what happened there? The first statement was a brush-off, but mirroring forced them to clarify what was really going on. If I'd taken their first answer at face value, I'd have missed a serious pain point.

Getting to the Core Issue

Prospect: *"My team isn't performing the way I need them to."*

Me: *"The way you need them to?"*

Prospect: *"Yeah, they're struggling to generate their own pipeline, and our close rates are lower than last year."*

What was a broad, fluffy statement (*"isn't performing"*) has now been broken down into two specific issues - pipeline generation and closing deals. Now I know exactly where to take the conversation.

How to Make Mirroring Even More Effective

- Use a slight upward tone. It should sound natural, not robotic or scripted.
- Don't overdo it. If you mirror after every sentence, you'll sound weird. Use it when a prospect gives a vague or interesting statement.
- Pair it with silence. After mirroring, shut up for a second. Most people can't stand silence, so they'll instinctively fill it with more information.

The Bottom Line

Most reps fire off question after question, racing through discovery as if they're working through a checklist. The best sellers know the real gold comes when you shut up and let the prospect do the talking. Mirroring is the easiest way to make that happen.

The next time a prospect gives you a vague or loaded statement, try mirroring it back and watch what happens. Nine times out of ten, they'll tell you exactly what you need to know without you even having to ask.

Labelling - Calling Out the Unspoken

Most reps listen to what a prospect is saying, but they completely miss *how* they're saying it: the hesitations, the pauses, and the moments where they almost say something, but hold back.

Labelling is about calling out what's beneath the surface. It's when you verbalise what you think the prospect is feeling, forcing them to either confirm or correct you.

And when you do it right, they'll almost always give you more than they intended to.

As a concept, labelling is a simple one. Instead of asking, *"Are you frustrated?"* (which sounds like an interrogation), you say, *"I get the sense you're frustrated."* That subtle shift makes a massive difference. The first version forces them to give a yes or no answer. The second makes them feel heard, which makes them double down and elaborate.

The more they elaborate, the more you learn. And the more you learn, the easier the deal gets.

Why Labelling Works So Well

1. **It makes the prospect feel like you get them.** People love feeling understood. Labelling shows you're paying attention beyond the words - you're picking up on their tone, their hesitation, their frustration.
2. **It gets past surface-level answers.** Prospects often downplay their problems because they don't want to sound like they're struggling. Labelling brings those struggles out into the open.
3. **It helps you qualify deals faster.** If a deal isn't real, labelling can clarify that sooner, before you waste time chasing something that isn't going to close.
4. **It positions you as an expert.** When you label correctly, you sound like someone who's seen this before which instantly builds credibility.

Here's some real examples from my discovery calls

Labelling Frustration

Prospect: *"I was promised I'd be hiring experienced sellers, but now I've got a team of graduates."*

Me: *"I can imagine that's frustrating."*

Prospect: *"Yeah, it's not what was agreed. Now I have to train them from scratch while still hitting the same targets."*

If I hadn't labelled what they had said, they might have brushed past this and kept things polite. But by calling out their frustration, I got them to double down on the pain, which makes for a much stronger sales conversation.

Labelling Hesitation

Prospect: *"The business brought in a new CRO who's completely derailed my plans."*

Me: *"I get the sense you're not too happy with this situation?"*

Prospect: *"I'm absolutely fuming. All the work I've put in just got thrown out the window."*

Me: *"Is it fair to say you're considering your position?"*

Prospect: *"That's a fair assumption."*

At this point, I knew that this VP might leave soon, which completely changed how I handled this opportunity. If I hadn't labelled their frustration, I'd have been wasting my time on a deal that was about to vanish.

Labelling Yourself - When You Don't Want to Assume

Sometimes, you sense frustration, hesitation, or doubt but you don't want to put words in their mouth. That's where labelling yourself comes in.

This is when you label how you would feel if you were them, making it safe for them to confirm (or correct) you.

For example, if a prospect tells me their sales team isn't hitting their targets, I might say:

"If that was me, I'd be a little worried. But I don't know, maybe you don't feel that way?"

This does two things:

1. It makes them feel safe about telling you more, because, instead of accusing them of feeling a certain way, I'm framing it as *how I would feel.*
2. This invites correction if they *don't* feel worried, in which case they'll tell me why. But most of the time, they'll agree and expand on just how much of a problem it really is.

Another example:

Prospect: *"We've had the same close rate for the past year, but we want to improve it."*

Me: *"I mean, if I was in your position, I'd be a bit frustrated. Or do you not see it that way?"*

This works because instead of forcing an emotion on them, I'm giving them permission to own or reject it. And once they do, I can go deeper.

Labelling the Boss - When You're Selling through Someone Else

Sometimes, you're selling to a champion - someone who loves what you're saying but isn't the final decision-maker.

A great way to test the waters is to label the boss.

Me: *"I'm just thinking through what your CFO might say if they were listening to this conversation. What do you think their main concerns would be?"*

This does two things:

1. It helps you understand what's going on internally. If they know what the CFO's concerns are, you now know what objections to prepare for.
2. It makes them feel like you're one step ahead. You're already thinking about how to help them sell this internally - which builds trust.

Another approach:

Me: *"I'm guessing that if your boss listened to this conversation, they'd agree with everything you've just said?"*

Prospect: *"Well... actually, they might push back on the pricing."*

Now I know exactly where the real challenge is, and I can address it before it kills the deal.

How to Make Labelling Even More Effective

- **Use a neutral tone.** This isn't about pushing or challenging - it's about surfacing real emotions.
- **Pause after labeling.** The prospect will almost always fill the silence.

- **Don't soften it too much.** Saying *"I could be wrong, but..."* weakens the label. Instead, be direct: *"I get the sense that..."* or *"It sounds like..."*

The Bottom Line

Labelling is one of those techniques that can feel unnatural at first but works like magic when you get it right.

Most reps are afraid to call things out. The best sellers? They have no problem putting words to the emotions sitting just beneath the surface.

The next time you sense frustration, hesitation, or doubt in your prospect's voice - label it.

Going Left

Ever heard the phrase "People want what they can't have."?

Well this is exactly what you can leverage if you get the sense that you're dealing with a passive prospect, and you want to test their desire.

Here's a quick story.

I was recently on a discovery call with a VP of Sales. I got the sense that, despite him sharing a fair amount of pain with me, this wasn't the biggest priority in his world. He had somewhat of a defensive appearance, and it felt like hard work to get him to show a level of enthusiasm in the conversation.

Me: *"I may be wide of the mark here Phil, but I'm getting the sense this is more of a "would be nice to fix" problem rather than a "need to fix quickly" problem. Would it make more sense for us to revisit this down the line?"*

At this point, Phil's whole demeanour changed.

Phil: *"Actually no, it really is key for me to fix this. Apologies if I hadn't made that clear. I'd like to set up another conversation and pull in my Rev Ops Leader too"*

This story is a prime example of using loss aversion and psychological reactance to gauge and influence a prospect's true level of interest. The fundamental idea at play is simple: when something is taken away - or even just the possibility of it - people tend to want it more. This technique subtly forces the prospect to re-evaluate their own priorities and clarify their level of interest.

The move that shifts the dynamic is what we can call "going left" - essentially, stepping away from the sale instead of going towards it. It's the precise opposite of what your prospect expects you to do.

In sales, "going left" refers to an intentional move away from traditional (and old-fashioned) persuasion tactics associated with sales, and instead leveraging scarcity, loss aversion, and power dynamics.

The Bottom Line

Many salespeople are fearful of using this kind of technique as it conflicts with their need for approval.

They are nervous about "calling out" their prospect's apparent lack of interest, in case it offends them or runs the risk of losing the sale.

In fact, when you are confident enough to "go left", it simply gives you more clarity on what is a real prospect and what isn't a true opportunity.

How to Avoid Being Dragged Into the Weeds

At some point in a discovery call, you will lose control. Examples include:

- The prospect starts going on a tangent for 10 minutes about something completely irrelevant.
- They bombard you with technical or product questions far too early.
- They take the conversation into the weeds of internal processes, edge cases, and minor details that don't move the deal forward.

If you let them, they'll waste half your call talking about things that won't actually help them make a decision.

Why This Happens

Prospects don't do this to be difficult. They do it because:

1. **They don't run sales calls - you do.** Prospects tend to talk about what's top of their mind, not what's actually relevant. If you don't take control, they will.

2. **They want to sound like they're in control.** Buyers love feeling like they're the expert in their world. When they start oversharing details about internal processes, legacy systems, or competitor comparisons, it's often just them flexing their knowledge.

3. **They're stalling**. Sometimes, a prospect will drag the conversation into the weeds because they're uncomfortable talking about their real problems. It's easier to talk about *"how we evaluate vendors"* than to admit *"our team is struggling, and it's hurting our revenue."*

Regardless of the reason, it's your job to get them back on track.

How to Take Back Control without Killing the Conversation

If you cut them off too aggressively, you'll come across as rude. If you let them ramble, you'll burn through your discovery call and learn nothing useful. They may also get annoyed you've not shared anything, despite them being the reason you ran out of time.

You need to reset the conversation without breaking rapport - here's how you do it:

Use Soft Interruptions to Pull Them Back

If they're waffling on about internal processes, gently steer them back:

"That's really helpful, William. I appreciate you sharing all of that. I'm just conscious of time, and I want to make sure we focus on what matters most. Can we bring it back to [pain point previously shared]?"

This works because:

- It acknowledges the point they previously shared (so they don't feel shut down and can see that you're trying to take them back to where they want help).
- It reframes the agenda so they remember why they're here.
- It keeps you in control, without being rude.

Other variations:

- *"That's useful context. Can I take us back to something you said earlier about [key pain point]?"*
- *"If we could just take a step back for a moment..."*
- *"Given what you shared at the start of the call about [key pain point], can we park that for a second and come back to it?"*
- *"Just to reset the conversation slightly..."*

Make Time Your Friend

Most people want to be seen as respectful of time. So when they start veering off course, remind them:

"I want to make sure we're using your time wisely. Let's refocus on [core issue]."

This subtly shifts them back without making them feel like they've been talking nonsense.

Flip It Back to Their Goal

If they're fixated on product details, internal workflows, or process-heavy discussions, flip the script:

"I totally understand why that's important. But I want to make sure we're focused on the main thing here - which I believe is solving [pain point]; is that fair?"

This forces them to remember why they booked the call in the first place.

When Prospects Ask Too Many Product Questions Too Early

Some prospects will try to turn the call into a demo before discovery is even done.

Prospect: *"Can you just show me how it works?"*
Me: *"Yes, of course; just before I do that, I want to make sure I'm actually showing you something that's relevant. Can I ask what specifically you are hoping to see today?"*

This does two things:

1. It makes them clarify what they actually want, instead of you guessing.
2. It lets you stay in control of the flow of the conversation.

The Golden Reset Line - When All Else Fails

If you feel like the call is going nowhere, here's your silver bullet:

"This has been helpful, but I just want to pause for a second. Based on everything we've discussed so far as opposed to the reasons you wanted to speak with me, I'm not totally sure we're covering the right area; is that fair?"

One of two things will happen:

1. They snap back to reality. *"Yeah, you're right - let's focus back on X."*
2. They reveal that they're not actually that serious. *"Honestly, we're just exploring right now."*

Either way, you get clarity and take back control.

What Happens When You Don't Take Control?

We've all had those calls. You hang up and think:

"What the hell just happened? I'm not even sure what the next steps are or why they'd buy"

You spent the entire time talking about their career to date, their company history, internal workflows, edge cases, and nonsense that didn't move the deal forward.

By the time you tried to steer it back, it was too late. The call ended, and you're stuck with a prospect who still hasn't admitted to having a real problem. This makes booking the next call so much harder as well, since the prospect has no clue if you can even help.

The Bottom Line

Most sales reps let prospects run the show and just hope for the best. The best reps? They don't let that happen, they lead every call with confidence - without being pushy.

The next time a prospect starts drifting, don't just sit there waiting for it to end. Steer the call back on course and make sure the conversation is moving the deal forward, not just filling time.

Being Silent - the Underrated Superpower

Most salespeople talk too much. Heck, most people do.

They ask a question, the prospect gives a half-answer, and, instead of letting it breathe, they jump in with another question or start talking to fill the space.

Big mistake.

Silence is one of the most powerful tools in a discovery call - when you use it properly. But most sales reps can't handle it. They can't keep quiet. Sitting in silence kills them.

The second they feel a gap in the conversation, they panic and start rambling. They re-explain something, they re-explain their question - "...the reason I ask is..." They throw in an extra question or, even worse. they answer their own question before the prospect has a chance to.

The best salespeople lean into the silence.

Why Silence Works

1. **It forces the prospect to keep talking.** People naturally want to fill awkward silences - if you stay quiet, they'll often give you far more information than they originally intended.
2. **It makes you seem more confident.** Ever notice how the most experienced people in any room don't rush to fill every silence? That's because they're comfortable. Silence makes you look in control.
3. **It prevents knee-jerk answers.** Prospects often give quick, surface-level answers to move the conversation along. When you stay silent, they'll reflect and give you a real answer.
4. **It makes you sound like you're actually thinking.** If you fire back responses too quickly, you sound scripted. If you pause before answering, you sound thoughtful and considered - which builds trust.

Where to Use Silence in Discovery Calls

There are a few moments where silence is particularly powerful:

After the Golden Minute

You ask, *"What's the main challenge you're dealing with right now?"*

They give a short answer. Most reps would immediately follow up with another question.

Don't.

Stay silent for 2-3 seconds.

Watch what happens.

The prospect will often feel the need to keep going - and that's when they give you the real answer, one that's actually helpful.

After a Tough Question

You ask, *"What happens if this problem doesn't get solved?"*

They pause.

You wait.

Most reps panic and in an attempt to soften it (because they're worried they've upset the prospect with their question). So they jump in with more details such as, *"I mean, does it cause issues for [X]?"*, or they even start to answer their own questions.

Now the prospect has an easy out; they can just say, *"Yeah, I suppose"* and move on or even worse, just use your answer as their answer. Now you've not learnt anything, you've just got your own answer to go on.

Use silence to make your prospect feel the weight of the question and give you a real answer.

After an Objection

Prospect: *"We're already doing something similar internally."*

Most reps immediately fire back with: *"I totally get that, but let me tell you why you need us..."*

Instead, just pause.

Silence makes the prospect feel that they need to explain more. They'll often continue:

"I mean, it's not the best, it's quite manual and time-consuming but it works"

Now you've got something to work with.

How to Train Yourself to Shut Up

If silence doesn't come naturally to you, here's how to start using it:

1. Count to Two in Your Head

When you ask a question, force yourself to count to two before saying anything else.

2. Mute Yourself on Zoom Calls

If you're doing a remote discovery call, mute yourself after you ask a question. You'll be shocked at how much more your prospects say when they don't hear you breathing, shifting, or jumping in too soon.

3. Pay Attention to When You're Interrupting

If you listen back to your own calls, you'll probably notice that you interrupt far more than you thought. The first step to fixing it is being aware of when you're doing it.

4. Sounds Daft, but Pinch Yourself.

When I realised how much I was interrupting I started to pinch myself on purpose every time I did it. It may sound daft, but it really worked for me.

The One Silence That Makes Prospects Sweat

If you really want to test yourself, try this:

After a prospect tells you their problem, simply say:

"That sounds tough."

Then say nothing.

Watch how they react.

They'll usually fill the silence by expanding on their challenge. And when they do? That's your real leverage.

What Happens When You Don't Use Silence?

Without pauses, you tend to rush through the call, the prospect will give surface-level answers, and you will never get to the real pain.

By the end of the conversation, you'll have a bunch of half-baked insights, but nothing that makes them actually want to buy.

And then you'll wonder why the deal isn't moving forward.

The Bottom Line

Most sales reps talk their way out of a deal.

The best ones shut up and let the prospect do the work.

Silence isn't awkward. Silence is pressure.

The next time you feel the urge to jump in and fill the gap - don't. Hold it. Let the prospect talk.

And when they do? They'll tell you what you need to know.

What to Do When Pushed for a Feature You Don't Have

At some point, a prospect is going to ask about something you don't have.

Maybe it's something you're planning to build, but it isn't live yet. Maybe it's something you'll never build because it's not part of your strategy. Either way, this moment can either kill the deal or move it forward, depending on how you handle it.

Most salespeople panic when this happens.

They either:

- **Overpromise** - "Yeah, that's on our roadmap!" (even when it's not. And, by the way, an experienced buyer doesn't like this answer as they know it'll be much further away than you're promising.)
- **Start defending** - "I'm not sure you'd actually need that feature because..."
- **Immediately fold** - "Yeah, we don't have that. Sorry."

None of these are good options.

The best sellers reframe the conversation so that the missing feature doesn't matter.

How to Handle it like a Pro

Before you answer, find out why they're asking. Here's an example:

Prospect: *"Does your product have a report that shows [X]?"*

Most sales reps will jump straight into an answer. Don't.

Instead, take control of the conversation:

You: *"that's interesting, help me understand how you'd use that report and what exactly you need"*

What this does:

- It forces them to explain why they care.
- It helps you figure out if this is a deal-breaker or just a passing thought.

- It buys you time to steer the conversation back to what actually matters.

Most of the time, when you ask this, the prospect will realise that the missing feature isn't actually that critical after all.

Redirect to the Core Problem

If the feature isn't critical, you can move the conversation back to more important issues.

You: "Got it. So if we solved [bigger pain point], would this still be a blocker for you?"

This makes them weigh up what's more important - the missing feature/report or actually solving their main challenge.

And most of the time, they'll move on.

If it is a Critical Feature, Position a Workaround

If the feature actually is important to them, you need to offer a different path.

Prospect: *"We really need this integration."*

Salesperson: *"Understood. A lot of teams we work with felt the same at first, but they've found that using [alternative method] gets them the same outcome. Would you be open to seeing how that could work for you?"*

This shifts the conversation from *"We don't have it"* to *"Here's how we solve that problem anyway."*

Most of the time, they'll be open to at least exploring the alternative, and now you're back in control.

If You *Know* the Feature Is Coming, Handle It Properly

Prospect: *"Do you support [X]?"*

You: *"Not today, but that's something we're actively working on for later this year. Out of curiosity, how soon would you need that in place?"*

This does two things:

- It confirms whether they actually need it now or if it's just a wish-list item.
- It stops you from making empty promises.

If they say, *"We'd need it straight away"*, you will know they're probably not a fit right now. But if they say, "It's something we'd like long-term, but it's not a deal-breaker," then you can keep things moving.

Never Just Say "No" and Leave It There

If a prospect asks about a feature you don't have, the worst thing you can do is just say, *"No, we don't support that."*

That's a conversation killer.

Instead, follow up with:

- *"Not today, but tell me more about why that's important to you?"*

- *"We don't have that at the moment, but how does it compare to what you're currently doing?"*
- *"I know that's something we've considered. Can I ask how you'd expect that to help with [main problem]?"*

This keeps the conversation moving and stops the missing feature from becoming the entire focus of the call.

The Wrong Way to Handle This

There are a few things you should never do in this situation.

Don't lie.

Saying *"It's coming soon,"* when it's not, will come back to bite you.

Don't get defensive.

If you start arguing about why they "don't really need it," you'll just make them double down on why they do.

Don't fold immediately.

If they ask about a feature you don't have and you instantly say, "No, we don't do that," you're handing them a reason to walk away. Push back. Dig deeper. Find out if it actually matters.

The Bottom Line

A missing feature doesn't lose deals. Not knowing how to handle it does.

When a prospect asks about something you don't have, take control of the conversation.

Most of the time, they'll realise it's not actually that important, or you'll be able to position a workaround.

And if it *is* a true deal-breaker? Better to find out now than after wasting weeks/months on a deal that was never going to close.

Adding Prospects to Alternative Platforms - Creating a Direct Line of Communication

Most salespeople rely too much on email.

They send a follow-up, wait days for a response, chase again, and wonder why things slow to a crawl.

The best sellers open up additional lines of communication.

One of the easiest and most effective ways to do this is by getting your prospects onto Slack.

Why This Works So Well

1. **Response speed skyrockets.** Emails sit in inboxes. Slack messages get answered. It is as simple as that.

2. **The relationship becomes more informal.** It moves you from *"a salesperson following up"* to *"someone they can quickly message when they need something."*
3. **You stay top of mind.** Instead of getting buried in a sea of emails, you're sitting right there in their Slack workspace.
4. **It removes friction.** If they need something, they don't have to open their inbox, search for your email, and reply. They just drop you a message.

How to Get a Prospect onto Slack

You don't need to overthink this. Just keep it casual:

"I'm guessing you use Slack? Why don't we connect there? It'll make it easier to keep in touch as we move forward."

If they say yes, now you've got a direct line - not just to them, but potentially to their wider team.

When to Do This

The best time to suggest Slack is as soon as the deal starts getting serious.

If you're sending over a proposal, setting up next steps, or needing to work through a final blocker, Slack makes a huge difference.

What If They Say No?

Not every company is open to this, and that's fine. If they say Slack isn't an option, try WhatsApp instead. The point is to find a faster, easier way to communicate than by email.

"No worries, do you use WhatsApp? Happy to drop you a message there so we're not just relying on email."

Most of the time, they'll be open to at least one of these options.

How This Helps Post-Sale

This isn't just useful for closing the deal. If they become a customer, having an open line of communication from day one can:

- Speed up onboarding.
- Make account expansion easier.
- Reduce churn because they actually talk to you instead of ghosting you.

The Bottom Line

If you're only using email to communicate with prospects, you're making life slower and harder for yourself.

Deals stall when communication slows. Getting a prospect onto Slack (or WhatsApp) keeps the momentum going and makes you the easiest vendor to work with.

Most salespeople don't do this. The ones who do win more deals, faster.

How to Close a Deal before the End of the Quarter

There's always a point in the sales cycle where timing becomes crucial.

Your manager is pushing to get deals closed before quarter-end. Finance is asking what's going to land. Your prospect is dragging their feet.

If you leave it up to them, the deal will slip into the next quarter - and remember, time kills deals anyway.

The best sellers take control of timing. They don't just "check in" and hope for the best. They ask the right questions early and set up the deal to close on their terms.

The Wrong Way to Create Urgency

Most salespeople screw this up.

1. **They push too hard too late.** If you only bring up timing when the quarter is ending, it's already too late.
2. **They throw out a blind discount.** *"If you sign by Friday, I can give you 10% off."*
   Now you've taught them that waiting gets them a better deal, and they also know if they ask for it after Friday you'll still honour it.
3. **They don't qualify timing early enough.** If you don't ask about their timeline until the end, you're just hoping it lines up with yours.

Hope is not a strategy.

How to Set Up a Timely Close without Sounding Desperate

Before you even get to closing, you need to know how serious they are and who's involved. So you need to ask the right questions up front.

Here's what to ask:

"What's the last possible date you'd need this in place by?"

Most reps ask, *"When would you like to have this in place?"* The prospect's answer is always *"as soon as possible"* or *"yesterday."* which are useless responses.

Flipping it to *"the last possible date"* forces them to think about their real timeline.

"Who in the business can kill this deal?"

If you don't know who can stop this from happening, you're blind. There is always someone who can sink this deal, so identify them early.

"What's happened in the past when your team has bought something like this? What did that process look like?"

Many buyers have never actually been through a purchasing process with their current company before (if at all). Asking this gives you an insight into their buying maturity and whether you'll need to guide them.

"If we don't get you up and running by [X date], what happens?"

If there's no real consequence to delaying, the deal will be delayed.

"What pushback do you expect from your boss?"

Get ahead of objections before they happen.

Make Them Sell the Deal Internally

When they say they need to run it by finance or leadership, make them do the work.

- *"Let's assume your CFO is on board. What's the reason you'd tell them we should move forward now?"*
- *"When you take this to [decision-maker], what questions do you think they'll ask you?"*

If they can't answer, they're not ready to sell it internally. Fix that first. Ask them, *"What do you need from me to help with this?"*

Never Just Offer a Discount - Make It Mean Something

Discounting isn't a strategy.

If you feel a discount is necessary to close the deal before quarter-end, don't just throw it out there. Instead, tie it to commitment.

"I don't even know if I can offer anything, but if I could find a way to make this work, are you saying you'd be ready to move forward before [date]?"

This forces them to commit before you put anything on the table.

If they say *"Yes, we'd sign if you can make it work,"* then you've got leverage.

If they say *"We'd still need more time,"* you've just saved yourself from needlessly cutting margins.

What to Do When They Say, "We'll Just Do It Next Quarter"

Some prospects will push everything to next quarter if you let them.

If they say, *"We'll look at this again next quarter,"* respond with: *"I get that. Just out of curiosity, what's going to be different in Q2 compared to now?"*

If they can't give you a real answer, they're just stalling.

You can follow up with:

"I know these things have a tendency to keep getting pushed back. If this doesn't happen now, is it fair to assume there's a real risk that it keeps getting delayed?"

This forces them to confront the fact that delaying usually makes things harder, not easier.

The Bottom Line

Deals don't slip because prospects don't want to buy. They slip because salespeople don't take control.

If you wait until the last week of the quarter to create urgency, you've already lost.

The best sellers set the right expectations from the start, qualify timing early, and make sure there's a real reason to close now, rather than later.

Key Takeaways

Mastering discovery isn't about following a script or memorising a checklist. It's about understanding how to run a conversation that actually moves a deal forward.

The difference between good and great isn't massive, dramatic changes. It's the small details - the fine margins - that separate the top sellers from everyone else.

- **Think like a doctor, not a salesperson.** Diagnose before you prescribe. Make the prospect feel understood before you ever mention a solution.
- **Use mirroring to unlock more insight.** Repeat their last few words and let them expand. Most prospects will tell you more than they intended - if you just give them the space.
- **Label unspoken issues.** Prospects won't always admit their pain up front. Call it out, and they'll either confirm or correct you - either way, you get closer to the truth.

- **Stay in control of the conversation.** If they start dragging you into the weeds, pull them back. Time is your most valuable asset - so protect it.
- **Embrace silence.** Most reps talk their way out of deals. The best ones shut up and let the prospect do the work.
- **Handle missing features with confidence.** Don't apologise. Don't overpromise. Find out why they're asking and reposition the conversation back to what matters.
- **Open up additional lines of communication.** Email slows deals down. Getting a prospect onto Slack or WhatsApp keeps up the momentum and makes it easier to close.
- **Control the timeline.** If you don't qualify timing early, you'll spend the last week of the quarter begging buyers to close deals. Ask the right questions up front and remove the reasons for delay before they happen.

Discovery is where deals are won or lost.

It's your job to make every conversation count.

Chapter Fourteen

The Deadly Sins of Discovery

At this stage, you'll know what makes a strong discovery call. But knowing what to do isn't enough. You also need to be crystal clear on what not to do - because even the best reps can sabotage a great discovery call by falling into bad habits.

We'd love to tell you there are just seven Deadly Sins of Discovery, as it would have been a nice title for this chapter, but frankly, there are too many we can't ignore. If we'd stuck to seven, we'd be absolving you of some of your sins - and we're not here to do that.

Some of these are common mistakes that ruin deals before they even start. Others are subtle killers - things that seem harmless in the moment, but that ultimately prevents you from getting the real insights you need.

Avoid these deadly sins, and you'll instantly separate yourself from the reps who are just going through the motions.

Making It All about You

One of the fastest ways to kill your 'likeability' on a discovery call is to make it about you instead of them.

It happens naturally, without you even realising it. You're not doing it because you're selfish - you're doing it because you're human.

This isn't a sales problem. It's a human problem. Once you're aware of it you'll see it happening every single day.

People instinctively try to connect with others by relating things back to themselves. It's humans trying to create that "same here", or "I'm just like you" feeling. Someone shares a story, and we respond with something similar from our own experience. We think we're showing empathy and building a connection, but what we're really doing is shifting the conversation back onto us.

Seriously, it happens all the time. Let me give you two examples

Going away?

Say you tell someone you're going to New York. If they've been, their immediate response is likely to be, "Oh, we've been, we love it; you have to go to this restaurant" - they think they're building a connection with you but what they've actually done is taken your moment and made it about them

Going to see a movie at the cinema?

If someone's already seen it, the first thing they'll tell you is what they thought of the movie.

It really does happen all the time, I have friends who I hope read this part of the book just to realise how annoying they are. No names.

When someone shares something, here's what you should do instead of making it about you - ask questions.

- *When do you go?*
- *Who are you going with?*
- *What are your plans?*
- *Ah nice, are you planning to go anywhere in particular?*
- *Who are you going with?*
- *What do you think is going to happen?*

As I say, it's a human problem and it bleeds into sales. In the small talk, a prospect tells you what they've been up to or what their plans are, and the salesperson can't wait to try and build rapport with them with a "same here" response.

It also happens later in the discovery calls. For instance, if a prospect tells you about a challenge they're facing, and, instead of asking more about it, you could respond with:

"Yeah, we see that all the time! Most companies we work with have the same issue, which is why our platform..."

You think you're demonstrating credibility. But to the prospect, it just sounds like you're not listening.

Unless they've asked about social proof they don't care that you've seen this problem before. They care about their own problems.

Why This Happens - the Human Instinct to Make It about Us

1. **We Think Relating Makes Us More Likeable**
   - ☐ When someone shares an experience, we assume that saying we've had a similar one will build rapport.
   - ☐ In normal conversations with friends you can get away with it, but when discovery calls are time-limited events, it can kill your conversations.

2. **We're Too Eager to Prove We Understand**
   - ☐ You hear a familiar problem and your brain instantly jumps to the solution.
   - ☐ You want to prove you've seen this before. But instead of getting more details, you cut them off.

3. **We Default to Talking About What We Know Best - Ourselves**
   - ☐ If you don't control it, your brain will always pull the conversation back into your comfort zone.
   - ☐ For most reps, that is talking about their product, their experience, and their other customers.

How This Shows Up in Small Talk

This problem starts long before you get into the sales conversation - it often happens in the first minute of small talk.

Example: The Travel Conversation

- **Prospect:** *"I'm heading to New York next week."*
- **Average rep:** *"Oh nice! I went last year - there's this great bagel place you should check out."*
- **Strong rep:** *"Nice! Who are you going with, and have you been before?"*

Both reps mean well. But the average rep shifts the focus onto their own experience. The strong rep keeps it on the prospect.

Now apply that to sales.

Example 3: The Sales Conversation

- **Prospect:** *"Yeah, we need to improve our upsell and cross sell rates."*
- **Average rep:** *"Yeah, we see that a lot! Most companies we work with struggle with it, which is why our platform helps with…"*
- **Strong rep:** *"Got it. What's making upsell and cross sell such a challenge right now?"*

Same mistake, different setting. The average rep hears upsell and cross sell and assumes they already know the problem. The strong rep stays curious and lets the prospect tell their own story.

Why Everyone's Favourite Subject is Themselves - and How to Leverage It

There's a reason people love talking about themselves: it feels good.

Studies have shown that, when people talk about themselves, their brain releases dopamine - the same chemical linked to pleasure and reward. That's why a great conversation leaves you feeling energised, and why you instinctively enjoy conversations where you do most of the talking.

And prospects are no different. When you let them talk, they feel in control, listened to, and important.

And if they feel like you genuinely care, they'll tell you everything you need to know to close the deal.

How to Use This in Discovery

1. **Make Them Feel Like the Expert**
   - ☐ Your job isn't to prove you're the expert. It's to make them feel like they are.
   - ☐ Ask questions that make them think deeply about their business.
2. **Use Their Own Words to Keep Them Talking**
   - ☐ If they say, *"Our pipeline is all over the place"*, don't jump in with a solution.
   - ☐ Instead, say *"All over the place?"* and let them expand.

3. Get Out of the Way
- ☐ The less you talk, the more they'll open up.
- ☐ When in doubt, just shut up and let them fill the silence.

The Bottom Line

Remember that it never has been about you and it never will be. Prospects aren't interested in your experiences. They're interested in their own.

The best reps understand that the fastest way to build trust isn't to relate everything back to themselves - it's to make the prospect feel like they are the most important person in the room.

And when you do that? They'll tell you exactly what you need to know to win the deal.

The Need for Approval - When Being Liked Gets in the Way of Selling

It's an uncomfortable truth: most reps want to be liked, or even loved by their prospects more than they want to be effective.

Sometimes they don't even realise it. But you can see it in the way they sell. They avoid tough questions. They hesitate to challenge. They nod along to vague answers instead of pushing for real insights. Instead of leading the conversation, they follow, hoping that being agreeable will somehow turn into a deal.

Why? Because deep down, they're scared. Scared that if they push too hard, they'll make the prospect uncomfortable. Scared that if they challenge, they'll create friction. Scared that, if they go too far, the prospect won't like them. So they keep the conversation easy, safe, and pleasant, forgetting that the real goal is to get to the truth.

And that's where they go wrong.

As we said, prospects don't buy because they like you. They buy because they trust you. And trust isn't built by nodding along and agreeing with everything they say. It's built by asking the hard questions, challenging assumptions, and guiding them towards clarity, even when it's uncomfortable.

It's a brutal reality in sales. The best reps aren't always the most liked. They're the ones who cut through the noise, dig deep into the real pain, and push prospects to think differently. The strongest sellers don't need approval. They don't need to be liked. If they do, they'll struggle to ask the right questions, challenge weak answers, and push back when needed. And if they need to be liked, or in the worst cases, loved, they'll never be able to sell consultatively, differentiate themselves, or win consistently.

The Data - Why This Matters

Objective Management Group (OMG) has conducted extensive research on sales performance, analysing data from over 2.5 million sales professionals. Their findings show a clear difference between top-performing reps and those who struggle. Specifically, the top 10% of salespeople score an average of 89% in the "Doesn't Need Approval" competency, whereas the bottom 10% average just 55%.

That's a massive gap. The best salespeople are almost twice as likely to be completely detached from the need for approval, while the weakest reps are still chasing validation. This isn't a minor detail - it's a fundamental difference in mindset that separates top performers from those who struggle to close.

The high achievers aren't sitting there worrying about whether the prospect likes them. They're focused on getting to the truth, challenging assumptions, and driving the deal forward.

The ability to detach themselves from the need for approval directly correlates with a rep's ability to challenge, differentiate, and ultimately close more deals. If you're prioritising being liked over being effective, you're already losing.

Why This Happens - the Human Instinct to Seek Approval

Just like the last sin, this isn't just a sales problem, it's also a human problem.

Deep in our psychological make-up, we're wired to want to be liked. It's. The moment we feel like we're at risk of making someone uncomfortable, our brain starts screaming: *"Stop, you're going to upset them!"*

And that's exactly what happens in discovery calls.

- A prospect gives a vague answer, and, instead of pushing for clarity, the rep just nods and moves on.
- A prospect hesitates on a question, and, instead of holding the silence, the rep jumps in to "help" them out.
- A prospect brushes off a key issue, and, instead of challenging them, the rep lets it slide because they don't want to seem pushy.

This is the rep's need for approval getting in the way of selling.

The truth? Prospects don't respect reps who just agree with everything they say. They respect the ones who push them to think differently.

What the Need for Approval Sounds Like

Example 1: Letting Vague Answers Slide

- **Prospect:** *"Yeah, the team is doing okay."*
- **Average rep:** *"Nice, that's good to hear."*
- **Strong rep:** *"What does okay mean?"*

The average rep accepts the answer and moves on. The strong rep wants clarity on what they mean by "doing okay".

Example 2: Avoiding Tough Questions

- **Prospect:** *"Yeah, we're pretty happy with how the sales team are performing."*
- **Average rep:** *"Ah nice; glad to hear they're doing well."*
- **Strong rep:** *"It's not often I hear a sales manager say they're happy with the team's performance; they usually want more. In that case should we revisit this conversation in six months or so?"*

That last question forces the prospect to either agree and qualify out, or justify why they should be speaking with you. It takes confidence to do this, but that is exactly what separates strong reps from weak ones.

Example 3: Avoiding Discomfort

- **Prospect:** *"We're just in research mode right now."*
- **Average rep:** *"Cool, I get it, would you like to see a demo then?"*
- **Strong rep:** *"Really? Out of all the things you can be doing, what's the reason you're in research mode now and not kicking the can down the road by six months?"*

Most reps are terrified to ask this because they think it could kill the deal. But if the deal is not real to begin with, you'd be better off knowing now than after months of chasing.

How to Fix It - Becoming Comfortable with Discomfort

1. **Push for Specifics**
   - ☐ Anytime a prospect gives a vague answer, call it out.
   - ☐ Instead of *"That makes sense,"* say, *"Help me understand"* or *"I'm a bit confused, what do you mean by that?"*

2. **Ask Questions That Force Clarity**
   - ☐ *"On a scale of 1 to 10, how big of a problem is this?"*
   - ☐ *"What happens if this doesn't get solved?"*
   - ☐ *"If you believed we had the right solution, are you ready to move forward or are you not there yet?"*

3. **Be Willing to Walk Away**
   - ☐ If they don't have a real problem, qualify out.
   - ☐ Your job isn't to be liked. Your job is to find out if there's a deal to be done.

Tip: when asking people to rate something on a scale of 1-10 most people will say 7 - never accept a 7. Say this *"when people give a 7/10 they typically mean 6 or 8 - which one are you?"* This will give you good insight into how they perceive the problem.

The Bottom Line

The need for approval kills deals, because it stops you from getting to the real truth.

If you want to be liked, go work in customer success. If you want to be respected and close bigger deals you need to get comfortable making people uncomfortable.

Surrendering Control - When You Let the Prospect Call the Shots

Discovery isn't just about asking the right questions - it's also about controlling the conversation. When you let the prospect dictate the flow of the call, you're no longer leading. You're reacting. And the second you become reactive, you're on the back foot, answering their questions, following their agenda, and losing your ability to guide them towards a real buying decision.

Surrendering control doesn't just slow deals down; it kills them completely. If you let your prospect control the call, they'll take you in circles, waste time, and leave you with no real next steps.

The best reps lead. They set the pace, they guide the discussion, and they make sure every minute of the call is spent moving the deal forward. Average reps? They let the prospect take over and hope something good comes from it. Spoiler: it rarely does.

The Four Biggest Ways Reps Lose Control in Discovery Calls

1. Letting the Prospect Take over the Agenda

You've set your plan for the call. You know what you need to uncover. Then, within seconds, the prospect flips it on you.

Example:

- **Prospect:** *"Before we dive in, let me tell you about our company and how we operate."*
- **Average rep:** *"Okay, sure!"* (Then they spend 15 minutes listening to their backstory.)
- **Strong rep:** *"While that may feel like a good idea, I'm conscious of time, I have done my pre call prep and feel for this conversation I have a good understanding of the business. Can I suggest we focus on [pain point]?"*

If you let them take the lead after the agenda it can be difficult to recover.

2. The "Tell Me What You Do" Trap

This is a classic way reps get forced into a premature pitch.

Example:

- **Prospect:** *"I know very little about your company; why don't you just tell me what you do."*
- **Average rep:** *"Sure! So we're a platform that helps..."* (Then they start pitching.)
- **Strong rep:** *"Definitely happy to explain, but before I do, what piqued your interest so I can answer appropriately?"*

If you launch straight into an explanation, you're playing their game, not yours.

3. Getting Stuck in Answer Mode

When some prospects ask a question, they will then go into question mode, firing off question after question, putting you on the back foot.

- **Prospect:** *"How do you compare to [competitor]?"*
- **Rep (answers question).**
- **Prospect:** *"Do you integrate with X?"*
- **Rep (answers question).**
- **Prospect:** *"What's your pricing?"*
- **Rep (answers question).**

Before you know it, you've spent 20 minutes answering questions, but you've learned nothing about them.

Ways to Break Out of Answer Mode:

- **Instead of just answering, flip it back to them.**
  - ☐ *"Good question - help me understand, what's the reason you ask?"*
- **Take control after a few questions.**
  - ☐ *"I can definitely run through all of your questions, but just so I give you what you need on this call, let's focus on {problem} you mentioned and take it from there, sound fair?"*

If they're in rapid-fire mode, you're being interrogated, not having a conversation. Shift the focus back to them.

4. Letting the Prospect Dictate Next Steps

Average reps let prospects tell them what to do next.

Example:

- **Prospect:** *"Just send me some info, and we'll get back to you."*
- **Average rep:** *"Sure, I'll get something over later today."*
- **Strong rep:** *"Happy to send some details, I can probably do that later today, if I can, how long do you need to read it?"* Then they set the next steps based on their timeframes.

If you let them get away with vague next steps, you're in chase mode and the deal is likely to die right there. Meanwhile it'll sit in your pipeline for months and months as you're chasing them.

Why Reps Surrender Control

1. **Fear of Being "Too Pushy"**
   - ☐ Reps worry that, if they push back, they'll seem aggressive...
   - ☐ ...but prospects actually respect reps who lead the conversation instead of just reacting.
2. **Need for Approval Kicking In**
   - ☐ This ties back to the previous sin. If you're desperate to be liked, you'll avoid any friction - even when it's necessary.

3. Thinking That "Next Steps" Will Just Happen on Their Own

- ☐ Reps assume that if a prospect is interested, the deal will move forward naturally.
- ☐ The reality? Deals stall when you don't take control.

How to Stay in Control without Sounding like a Pushy salesperson

1. Redirect Gently, but Firmly

- ☐ If they try to hijack the agenda, acknowledge their point but pull it back.
- ☐ *"That's great context, but before we go there, what's made you look at this now?"*

2. Never Accept "Send Me Some Info" at Face Value

- ☐ If they ask for details, tie it to a timeframe and then get commitment based on that timeframe.

3. Push for Clear Next Steps

- ☐ Average reps let the call end on a vague note.
- ☐ Strong reps get commitments. *"What needs to happen on your side for this to move forward?"*

The Bottom Line

The second you give up control, you're just another salesperson waiting for a call back that will never come.

Take control. Guide the conversation. And never, ever let a prospect dictate the next steps. That's your job.

Getting Stuck in "Yes Mode" - When You Stop Selling and Start Agreeing

Most sales reps think they're good listeners. They believe they're building rapport, making prospects feel comfortable, and keeping the conversation flowing smoothly. In reality, many of them aren't actually listening at all - they're just agreeing, and waiting to speak.

This is "Yes Mode".

Instead of challenging, clarifying, and digging deeper, reps get stuck nodding along, saying *"That makes sense,"* or *"Yeah, I hear that a lot."* It feels like they're keeping the conversation positive, but what they're actually doing is avoiding the real issues the prospect is facing.

A prospect makes a vague statement, and, instead of pushing for clarity, the rep just agrees and moves on. The result? They never uncover the real pain, the deal stalls, and they walk away thinking it was a "great conversation" when, in reality, it was just a polite back-and-forth with no real progress.

What Yes Mode Sounds Like in a Discovery Call
Taking Surface-Level Answers at Face Value
Example:

- **Prospect:** *"Yeah, our team is struggling with pipeline right now."*

- **Average rep:** *"Got it. Yeah, I hear that a lot."*
- **Strong rep:** *"Struggling in what way?"* And. if they get a vague answer back, they dig deeper: *"When people say 'struggling', they tend to mean one of two things. Either they're not generating enough pipeline, or not converting at the necessary level - which one is it for you?"*

You see how the average rep accepts the answer and moves on. The top rep digs deeper to get to the real issue.

Avoiding the Tough Questions

Example:

- **Prospect:** *"We'd like to improve our close rate."*
- **Average rep:** *"Yeah, I totally understand."*
- **Top rep:** *"When you say 'improve,' what does that actually mean?"*

If you don't challenge vague statements, you'll never get to the real problem. And if you don't know the real problem, you're selling blind.

Why Reps Get Stuck in Yes Mode

1. **They Mistake Agreement for Good Rapport**
   ☐ They think that nodding along builds trust, whereas real trust comes from understanding, not just agreeing.

2. They Fear Breaking the Flow of the Conversation

☐ They worry that pushing for clarity will make things awkward, whereas, in reality, it's what leads to real insights.

3. They're Too Focused on Keeping It "Positive"

☐ The goal of discovery isn't to have a nice chat. It's to find out if there's a real problem worth solving.

Ways to Break Out of Yes Mode and Take Control

1. Force Yourself to Ask "How" or "Why" After Every Key Statement

☐ If a prospect says *"We're struggling with X,"* your immediate response should be to ask either what struggling means, or why they're struggling.

2. Repeat Their Own Words Back to Them

☐ If they say *"We need more pipeline,"* respond with *"How much more?"* and let them expand on the point.

3. Call Out When Something Doesn't Add Up

☐ If they say *"We're happy with our current provider,"* but they booked a call with you, ask *"Just so we're on the same page, and I trust you'll take this question in the ways its intended but, if you're happy, what's the reason you wanted to speak with me today?"*

The Bottom Line

Agreeing with everything a prospect says might feel like good selling, but it's actually the opposite. The best reps know that deals aren't won by agreeing. They're won by uncovering the truth.

Push deeper. Challenge assumptions. Stop nodding along and start selling.

Happy Ears - Being Content with Surface-Level Pain and Commitment

As we said, many reps suffer from having "happy ears"

i.e., hearing what sounds like pain. The moment a prospect says, *"Yeah, we're struggling with this,"* they think, *"Great, I've got my in."* But not all pain is created equal. If you settle for surface-level problems, you'll never uncover the deep, compelling reason they need to buy.

When it comes to commitment, a rep hears something that sounds positive and assumes it means a deal is happening. It's not just about accepting shallow pain points, but also about hearing signs of interest and mistaking them for real commitment.

Average reps take what they hear at face value. Strong reps push further to uncover urgency and true intent.

What Happy Ears Sound Like in a Discovery Call

Accepting a Vague Problem as a Real Problem

Example:

- **Prospect:** *"Yeah, our team isn't hitting target."*
- **Average rep:** *"Got it. So it sounds like you need help improving win rates?"*
- **Strong rep:** *"What's stopping them from hitting target?"*

The average rep is content with what they've heard. The strong rep gets specific about the reason why they're not hitting targets.

Assuming a Problem is Big Enough to Matter

Example:

- **Prospect:** *"We'd like to improve efficiency."*
- **Average rep:** *"Of course, efficiency is important."*
- **Strong rep:** *"Like to improve it, or need to improve it?"*

A problem they'd *like* to fix is not the same as one they *need* to fix.

Hearing Interest and Mistaking It for Commitment

Example:

- **Prospect:** *"Yeah, this looks really interesting."*
- **Average rep:** *"Awesome! I'll send over some details."*

- **Strong rep:** *"And so I don't get happy ears, what specifically is interesting about this to you?"*

Interest is not intent. Average reps get excited. Strong reps test it.

Why Reps Suffer With Happy Ears

1. **They're Desperate for a Win**
   - ☐ They hear what they *want* to hear instead of what's actually being said.
2. **They Mistake Pain for Urgency'**
   - ☐ The mere fact they have a problem doesn't mean they're ready to fix it.
3. **They Mistake Interest for Commitment**
   - ☐ Just because they like what they see, it doesn't mean they're ready to buy.
4. **They Avoid Difficult Conversations**
   - ☐ Asking for more info and getting a prospect to commit to their answers is uncomfortable. That is down to a need for approval kicking in.

Ways to Stop Getting Happy Ears and Start Selling

1. **Push for Specifics**
   - ☐ If they say *"Our team isn't hitting their targets,"* ask *"What's the reason they're not?"* and *"How long has this been the case"* along with *"What have you done to try to solve this"*

2. **Quantify the Problem**
   - ☐ *"In pounds and pence how much are they short of target each month?"*
   - ☐ *"Is that a lot of money for the business?"*
   - ☐ *"How much longer can this go on for?"*
3. **Test for Real Commitment**
   - ☐ *"Is this not something you can fix yourself?*
   - ☐ *"Why don't you wait another six months, maybe this will fix itself?"*
   - ☐ *"Is this something you'd like to solve, or is it something you need to solve?"*
4. **Challenge Their Priorities**
   - ☐ *"Out of everything you're dealing with, where does this rank in importance?"*
   - ☐ *"Who else cares about this?"*
   - ☐ *"Do they know we're speaking and that you're actively looking for help?"*

The Bottom Line

Just because a prospect has a problem, it doesn't mean they're going to buy. Average reps hear surface-level pain and interest and assume they have a deal. Strong reps push further, challenge priorities, and uncover real urgency and commitment.

Not Qualifying Out - Wasting Time on the Wrong Deals

Most reps have inflated pipelines. They live in hope and therefore hate to mark an opportunity as "closed lost" in the CRM unless the prospect has specifically said "it's over" - the best reps don't live in hope. Instead, they prefer to spend their time with people who want to buy so they qualify out, hard. They are ruthless.

When you don't qualify out early, you waste time chasing prospects who were never going to buy in the first place.

You spend months on "opportunities" that were dead on arrival, instead of focusing on the ones that you can close.

Average reps think every conversation is a potential deal. Strong reps actively disqualify prospects who aren't serious.

What Not Qualifying Out Sounds Like in a Discovery Call

1. Mistaking Interest for Intent

Example:

- **Prospect:** *"Yeah, this looks interesting."*
- **Average rep:** *"Great! Let's book another call to go deeper."*
- **Strong rep:** *"I often hear that, but, so that I don't make assumptions, what's interesting about this to you?"*

Interest doesn't equal urgency. The average rep assumes interest means intent. The strong rep pressure-tests it.

2. Avoiding Hard Qualifying Questions

Example:

- **Prospect:** *"We're just exploring options right now."*
- **Average rep:** *"Got it! Happy to walk you through everything."*
- **Strong rep:** *"Out of all the things you could spend your time on, what's making you explore them today, with me?"*

If they're *just looking*, you need to know if they'll ever be *ready to buy.*

3. Letting a Deal Drag On Without Clear Next Steps

Example:

- **Prospect:** *"We need to think about this internally."*
- **Average rep:** *"No worries, I'll check in next week."*
- **Strong rep:** *"Who else cares about this internally and what do you need to do to be ready to proceed with conversations?"* Then they ask for timeframes and a commitment to speaking in-line with those timeframes.

If you're leaving a call without clear next steps, you're just adding dead weight to your pipeline.

Why Reps Struggle to Qualify Out

1. **Big Pipelines Make Them Feel Better**
   - ☐ They think they look better internally because they have a bigger pipeline and more potential deals = more chances of closing. They live in hope.
2. **They're Afraid of Hearing "No"**
   - ☐ They avoid tough questions because they don't want to disqualify a prospect too soon. Again, they are living in hope.
3. **They Mistake Long Sales Cycles for Progress**
   - ☐ Just because someone is *still talking* to you, it doesn't mean they're *getting closer* to buying.

How to Qualify Out Without Killing Good Deals

1. **Ask "Why Now?" and Challenge the Answer**
   - ☐ *"What happens if you don't solve this?"*
   - ☐ *"What's making this compelling to solve now?"*
   - ☐ *"What's the reason you aren't kicking this can down the road?"*
   - ☐ *"Is solving this a want or a need?"*
2. **Test for Real Decision-Making Power**
   - ☐ *"Who else cares about solving this?"*
   - ☐ *"Who else would feel left out if you made a purchase and didn't include them?"*
   - ☐ *"Whose signature would be on the order form?"*

- [ ] *"Has a budget already been allocated for this?"*
- [ ] *"Who can stop this deal from happening?"*

The Bottom Line

Average reps are hopeful sellers; they chase every deal. Strong reps know when to walk away. They enjoy qualifying out.

If you don't qualify out early, your pipeline fills up with ghosted prospects, endless follow-ups, and deals that will never close. Be ruthless. If there's no compelling reason and urgency you're better off qualifying out and moving on.

"Competitor Reflux" - Reacting Instead of Controlling the Conversation

The moment a competitor's name comes up, most reps panic. They feel like they've been put on the spot, so they go straight into defense mode, rattling off why their solution is better. Or worse, they get flustered, try to avoid the question, and lose credibility.

This is "Competitor Reflux" - the knee-jerk reaction to jump into comparisons the second a competitor is mentioned.

Average reps get defensive and start pitching. Strong reps stay neutral instead; they keep their cool, ask questions and gather information.

What Competitor Reflux Sounds Like in a Discovery Call

Jumping Straight Into Battle Mode

Example:

- **Prospect:** *"How do you compare to [Competitor]?"*
- **Average rep:** *"Oh, we're much better because..."* (Launches into a feature war.)
- **Strong rep:** *"Good question. What are your main requirements when it comes to finding a solution and I'll share how we stack up?"*

The average rep assumes they need to defend themselves.

The strong rep slows down and finds out why the prospect cares.

Trash-Talking the Competition

Example:

- **Prospect:** *"We're currently using [competitor]."*
- **Average rep:** *"Oh yeah, a lot of our customers switched from them because of [reason]"*
- **Strong rep:** *"Interesting, I'm guessing you're really happy with them, so what's the reason we're speaking?"*

If they're *already using* a competitor, you don't need to tell them what's wrong with it. Let them tell you, then you can use their words against the competitor, not yours.

Why Reps Struggle With Competitor Reflux

1. **They Feel Like They Have to Win the Argument**
   - ☐ The goal isn't to prove you're "winning" It's to understand the prospect's decision-making process.

2. **They Assume the Competitor Is the Real Obstacle**
   - ☐ Most deals aren't lost to competitors. They're lost to indecision.

3. **They Get Emotionally Attached**
   - ☐ You're not competing against the competitor. You're competing for clarity.

How to Handle Competitor Mentions like a Pro

1. **Stay Neutral and Ask "Why"**
   - ☐ *"What's making you look at them?"*
   - ☐ *"What do you like about them?"*
   - ☐ *"What's missing?"*

2. **Flip the Conversation Back to Their Needs**
   - ☐ *"What's going to be the deciding factor?"*
   - ☐ *"How will you know when you've found the right provider?"*

3. **Don't Get Defensive - Get Curious**
   - ☐ If they mention they're working with a competitor, don't flinch. Just ask: *"What's your experience been with them so far?"*
   - ☐ If they say they've already looked at a competitor, just ask *"How come you didn't sign up with them?"*

The Bottom Line

Competitor mentions aren't threats - they're opportunities.

Average reps react emotionally and start pitching. Strong reps stay calm, get curious, and use the moment to uncover what really matters to the prospect.

Control the conversation; don't let the competition control you.

Poor Time Management - Manage It like a Call of Four Quarters

Time is the most valuable asset on a discovery call, yet **average reps** waste it. They either spend too much time on small talk, rush through discovery, or leave no time to set next steps. By the end of the call, they're scrambling. Strong reps, on the other hand, manage their calls with precision.

A good discovery call should run like a game of American football - split into four quarters, each with a distinct purpose. If you don't control the clock, you'll run out of time before you get the commitments you need.

The Four Quarters of a Discovery Call

1st Quarter: Small Talk + the Golden Minute (0-4 Minutes)

This is where you set the tone. You don't need 10 minutes of small talk, but skipping it entirely makes the conversation feel transactional. The key is to be intentional and transition smoothly into discovery.

Outcome: You build rapport without wasting time and get straight to the reason they're here.

2nd Quarter: Deep Discovery (5-15 Minutes)

Now it's time to gather information (not give it!). This is where the real value of the call comes from - uncovering pain, priorities, and decision drivers. Average reps ask checklist questions. Strong reps challenge, clarify, and uncover urgency.

Outcome: You move beyond surface-level pain and find the real problem that needs solving.

3rd Quarter: Digging Deeper + Handling Objections (16-25 Minutes)

By this stage, you should have real insights, but now you need to refine them. This is where you clarify objections, qualify decision-makers, and test urgency. Average reps skip this and go straight to pitching. It's where they're most comfortable - strong reps keep control and challenge assumptions.

Outcome: You gain a deeper understanding of their real problem and why it matters, as well as addressing objections and ensuring they're serious about solving their problem.

4th Quarter: Next Steps + Timeline Commitment (26-30 Minutes)

This is where average reps lose deals - they run out of time, rush through next steps, and leave with weak commitments. Strong reps manage the clock and lock in clear next steps.

Outcome: You leave the call with clear, committed next steps instead of vague promises.

Why Reps Struggle With Time Management

1. **They Don't Set an Agenda**
   - ☐ If you don't control the flow, the prospect will do it.
2. **They Let the Prospect Ramble**
   - ☐ If they go off-topic, strong reps redirect: *"That's useful context, but let's focus on..."*
3. **They feel like they need to share everything**
   - ☐ Average reps have a fear that, by not discussing every single way they can help. they'll not get the prospect excited enough to come back. All you need to focus on is their biggest problem and the best way you can help. The rest will come out in further conversations.
4. **They Run Out of Time for Closing**
   - ☐ They never leave enough time to agree on the next steps so are always rushing in the final minutes. This can end in the prospect having to leave the call and agreeing to find a time over email - and we all know how that plays out.

How to Manage the Clock like a Pro

1. **Set the Agenda Right Away**
   - ☐ With a clear goal that, by the end of the call, you'll either be saying "thanks but no thanks" or booking in more time.

2. **Do a proper time check**
   - ☐ *"We've got this in for 30 minutes. Just so I understand, and no wrong answers, but when you look at your calendar, how are you for time today?"*

3. **Control the Conversation**
   - ☐ If they go off track say, *"That's helpful, but let's bring it back to..."*

4. **Always Leave 4 Minutes for Next Steps**
   - ☐ *"Before we wrap up, let's compare calendars and find a time to continue the conversation."*

The Bottom Line

If you don't control the time, you don't control the call. Average reps run out of time before getting what they need. Strong reps structure their calls like four quarters - so they always finish strong.

Run your call like a game, and win every quarter.

"Premature Pitchulation" - Pitching Too Soon and Losing the Deal

Most reps can't wait to pitch. The moment they hear a problem - *boom* - they're diving straight into why their product is the perfect solution. The issue? They haven't earned the right to pitch yet. They're pitching before they fully understand the problem, before the prospect is emotionally invested, and before they've built enough urgency to make it land.

Average reps suffer from "Premature Pitchulation" - they hear a trigger word and pounce. Or their need for approval kicks in and, instead of asking questions, they go into pitch mode. It's where they feel safe. They've delivered their pitch hundreds of times, so it's the easy option. Strong reps wait; like doctors, they continue to gather information and only diagnose, and prescribe when they know what the prospect needs.

What Premature Pitchulation Sounds Like in a Discovery Call

1. Pitching the Second They Hear a Problem

Example:

- **Prospect:** *"I'm struggling with pipeline visibility."*
- **Average rep:** *"Got it! Our platform has real-time dashboards that give you complete visibility."*
- **Strong rep:** *"What is it you're unable to see?"* Then they will explore why they need to see it and what visibility will enable them to do.

The average rep jumps in too fast. The strong rep holds back and gets to the root cause.

2. Pitching Before the Prospect Feels the Pain

Example:

- **Prospect:** *"Yeah, forecasting could be better."*
- **Average rep:** *"Our AI-driven forecasting tool fixes that completely."*
- **Strong rep:** *"Could be better how?"*

Strong reps keep going until they understand if the pain is real or not.

3. Pitching Before the Prospect is Emotionally Invested

Example:

- **Prospect:** *"We're looking at a few options."*
- **Average rep:** *"Well, let me tell you why we're the best option."*
- **Strong rep:** *"How will you know when you've found the right one?"*

The average rep assumes they're in a product comparison. The strong rep turns it into a deeper conversation, understanding what they're really looking for.

Why Reps Pitch Too Soon

1. They Mistake Interest for Readiness

☐ A prospect may say they have a problem and sound interested but, unless you truly understand the problem, you're pitching blind, the more you know the more specific you can be.

2. **They Want to Show Value Immediately**
   - ☐ But value is only clear when it's tied to the prospect's actual pain.

3. **It's Easy and Safe**
   - ☐ Rather than asking more questions, which become deeper and tougher as the call goes on, they avoid the harder questions and go to what they know, their pitch. Then they hope the prospect hears something and self-diagnoses.

4. **They Fear Losing the Opportunity**
   - ☐ They pitch early, hoping to "hook" them - when in reality, they're sounding like every other salesperson and pushing the prospect away.

Ways to Avoid Premature Pitchulation

1. **Hold Back and Diagnose First**
   - ☐ If they say *"We struggle with X"*, ask, *"What in particular are you struggling with?"* before pitching anything.

2. **Make Them Feel the Pain**
   - ☐ *"What's actually happening as a result of that?"*
   - ☐ *"What will happen if it continues this way?"*

3. **Wait for Them to Ask**
   - ☐ What you want is to hear, *"How do you help with that?"* That's your ticket to pitch. But don't do a feature dump; pitch in a

story that relates to what you've heard and use their language.

The Bottom Line

Premature pitching doesn't make you stand out - it makes you sound like every other salesperson. Average reps hear a keyword, panic, and default to their pitch, hoping something sticks. Strong reps stay in control, keep the prospect talking, and only prescribe a solution once they fully understand the problem.

If the prospect hasn't asked, *"How do you help with that?"*, then you're pitching too soon. Hold back, dig deeper, and let them invite you to sell.

Not Using Their Language Back - Missing the Emotional Impact

Prospects don't just give you any words - they give you theirs. How they describe their challenges, frustrations, and goals is exactly how they think about them. Average reps listen but rephrase everything into their own words. Strong reps mirror the prospect's exact language, reinforcing their pain and making them feel truly heard.

When you reframe their words and use yours, you dilute the emotional impact. If a prospect says, *"We feel betrayed by our vendor,"* and you later say, *"So you're a bit unhappy with them,"* you've completely softened the intensity of their pain.

What Not Using Their Language Back Sounds Like in a Discovery Call

1. Softening Their Pain

Example:

- **Prospect:** *"We're drowning in admin work."*
- **Average rep:** *"Spending too much time on admin, nobody wants that!"*
- **Strong rep:** *"You said you're drowning in admin, what does that mean in reality?"*

The average rep weakens the emotion of the problem. The strong rep amplifies it.

2. Replacing Their Words with Generic Business Jargon

Example:

- **Prospect:** *"Our sales process is a complete mess."*
- **Average rep:** *"Got it, so you need to optimise it?"*
- **Strong rep:** *"You said it's a complete mess - it's an interesting phrase, but help me understand, what does 'complete mess' actually mean?"*

If they say *mess*, use *mess*. If they say *chaos*, use *chaos*. Don't turn raw emotion into generic corporate language.

3. Missing the Underlying Emotion

Example:

- **Prospect:** *"Our team is completely demoralised."*
- **Average rep:** *"Sounds like morale is a little low."*
- **Strong rep:** *"Demoralised is a strong word, tell me more!"*

The average rep downplays it. The strong rep leans into it and gets to the root of the issue.

Why Reps Struggle to Mirror Language

1. **They Default to Their Own Script**
   - ☐ They have set phrases in their head and automatically revert to them.
2. **They Think Mirroring Sounds Unnatural**
   - ☐ In reality, it makes the prospect feel like they're truly being heard.
3. **They Don't Realise How Important It Is**
   - ☐ The words a prospect uses reveal what *actually* matters to them.

How to Start Using Their Language Back

1. **Repeat Their Exact Words**
   - ☐ If they say *"We're drowning"*, don't change it to *"...spending too much time"*. Keep it the same.
2. **Dig Deeper into Emotionally Charged Words**
   - ☐ *"You said it's a nightmare, what do you mean/tell me more?"*

☐ *"Frustrating in what way?"*

3. Use Their Language in Your Pitch

☐ When you finally pitch, reflect their words back to them. *"Earlier, you said you were drowning in admin - here's how we help with that"*

The Bottom Line

Average reps change a prospect's words and lose the emotional impact. Strong reps mirror their language and reinforce urgency. The better you reflect their pain, the more they'll feel like you actually understand it.

Speak their language, not yours.

Not Being Yourself - The Fastest Way to Lose Trust

About five years ago I'd occasionally be told, "You're very polished" by my prospects - and it bugged me. I never had the stones to ask what they meant because, deep down, I knew. They were saying I came across as rehearsed and too smooth, which I knew could suggest a lack of authenticity.

The second you sound "polished", or even scripted, you start to erode trust. Prospects can tell when you're putting on a "sales persona." They hear it in your voice, in the way you phrase things, and in how your energy shifts the moment the call starts. Nobody trusts a salesperson who sounds like they're acting.

Average reps follow a rehearsed script. Strong reps bring their real personality to every call.

What Not Being Yourself Sounds Like

1. Changing Your Tone the Second the Call Starts

Example:

- **Before the call:** Relaxed, natural, and engaging.
- **During discovery:** Stiff, overly polished, robotic.
- **Fix:** Keep your tone natural and consistent.

2. Sounding Overly Formal or Corporate

Example:

- **Prospect:** *"So tell me about your solution."*
- **Average rep:** *"Certainly. Our cutting-edge platform enables seamless integration across multiple environments..."*
- **Strong rep:** *"right, where to begin - the simplest way to explain it is..."*

If you wouldn't say it in a normal conversation, don't say it in sales. Be yourself.

Why Reps Struggle to Be Themselves

1. They Think "Professional" Means Stiff

☐ The best reps sound human, not robotic. They're not afraid to show off their personality.

2. **They Overthink Every Word**
    - ☐ Instead of having a conversation and treating it like one human speaking to another, they see it as a conversation between a true salesperson and a true buyer.
3. **They Try Too Hard to "Perform" Instead of Connect**
    - ☐ While sales is about presenting your best self, it's not a complete act - there is a bit of acting, but it's also about being seen as a consultative, trusted advisor who can guide the prospect to the right solution.

How to Sell Like a Human

1. **Talk Like You Normally Talk**
    - ☐ If you wouldn't say it in real life, don't say it in sales.
2. **Have a Personality**
    - ☐ Prospects lean into authenticity; it helps them feel more comfortable, so they open up.
3. **Make It a Real Conversation**
    - ☐ The best calls don't feel like sales calls. They're real conversations.

The Bottom Line

Average reps put on a "sales voice" and lose credibility. Strong reps sell in their own voice and thus build real trust and respect. If you sound different on a sales call than you do in real life, you're doing it wrong.

My Nan used to say *"I'd rather be disliked for who I am than liked for who I'm not"* and I live by that.

Asking Checklist Questions Instead of Having a Conversation

Discovery isn't an interview. But average reps treat it like one, running through a list of pre-written questions without truly engaging. Strong reps make it a conversation - reacting, adapting, and digging deeper based on what they hear.

What Checklist Discovery Sounds Like

Example:

- **Average rep:** *"What's your biggest challenge?" "What's your budget?" "What's your timeline?"*
- **Strong rep:** *"You mentioned your pipeline is down - what's the reason for that?" "How long has that been the case?" "What have you done to try and solve it?" "Why didn't that work?"*

One feels robotic. The other feels natural and engaging.

Why Reps Default to Checklist Mode

1. **They Think It Covers Everything**
   ☐ But a script can't uncover the real pain if you're not reacting to the answers.
2. **They're Afraid of Going Off-Script**
   ☐ The best discovery calls go beyond the surface-level questions.

3. **They Prioritise Efficiency Over Depth**
   - ☐ Fast questions don't mean fast deals. Deep questions create urgency.
4. **They're too afraid**
   - ☐ They are too afraid to react to what they've heard and ask a tough question. They still have a need for approval.

How to Ditch the Checklist and Have a Real Conversation

1. **Listen for Cues and Dig Deeper**
   - ☐ If they say, *"Closing deals is tough right now,"* don't just move on. Ask *"What do you mean by tough right now?"*
2. **React, Don't Just Ask**
   - ☐ Show you're engaged: *"That's interesting, tell me more - why do you think that is?"*
3. **Challenge Them Instead of Just Collecting Info**
   - ☐ *"You said you need to improve rep performance - just to clarify the language there, is it a need or more of a want?"*

The Bottom Line

Average reps check boxes. Strong reps create conversations that uncover real problems. If you're just running through a list, you're not doing discovery, you're just gathering surface level answers.

Combining Discovery with Demo - But It's Okay to Show "Something"

Old-school sales training says: *"Never show the product in discovery."* But prospects today often expect to see *something* early on. The mistake? Average reps turn discovery into a full-blown demo, and thus lose control of the conversation. Strong reps use quick, focused demos to reinforce discovery and excite the prospect, teasing them into the next. By doing this, they never let them replace discovery.

Where Reps Get This Wrong

Example:

- **Prospect:** *"Can you show me how it works?"*
- **Average rep:** *"Sure!"* (Launches into a 25-minute product walkthrough.)
- **Strong rep:** *"I'm happy to show something, but I'm conscious of time and therefore want to focus on the right thing. What are you most interested in seeing?"*

One gives up control. The other keeps the demo tied to real pain.

Why Reps Over-Demo Too Soon

1. **They Think the Product Will Sell Itself**
   - ☐ But without real pain, a demo is just a *tour* - not a reason to buy.
2. **They Want to Please the Prospect**
   - ☐ Instead of keeping control, they are saying

"Yes" to everything. You guessed it - this is down to the need for approval.

3. **They Confuse Interest With Urgency**
   - ☐ Just because they *want* to see it, that doesn't mean they're ready to buy.
4. **It's the Safe Option**
   - ☐ Most reps have run the demo hundreds of times; so it's easier than asking the tough questions.

How to Show Just Enough without Losing Control

1. **Tie the Demo to Their Specific Pain**
   - ☐ *"You mentioned that a lack of inbound demos is an issue - let's focus on that today and next time we speak I can show you the rest"*
2. **Keep It Short and Interactive**
   - ☐ *"I'll show you this part quickly - and then on the next call we can take a deeper look"*
3. **Never Let the Demo Take Over the Call**
   - ☐ If they ask for more, push back: *"Happy to go deeper, but I don't want to give you a harbour tour, there's a bit more I need to understand first and, from there, we can dive back in. We can always set up another call to go through it as well."*

The Bottom Line

Average reps let demos hijack discovery. Strong reps use demos as a tool to reinforce pain and tease the next steps - without letting the product do all the talking. If you're going to show something, make sure it's *strategic*.

Waiting to Speak vs. Actually Listening

Most reps think they're great listeners. In reality, the average ones aren't listening at all - they're just waiting for their turn to talk. Strong reps absorb what's being said, process it, and respond in a way that moves the conversation forward.

What Waiting to Speak Sounds Like

Example:

- **Prospect:** *"Our close rates have been dropping the last two quarters."*
- Average rep: *"Got it. So let me tell you how we can help with that..."*
- Strong rep: *"Why do you think that's happening?"*

One assumes. The other digs deeper.

Why Reps Struggle to Truly Listen

1. **They're Focused on Their Next Question**
   - ☐ And they do this instead of responding to what's actually being said.

2. They Want to Sound Smart and Show They Know the Answer

☐ So they jump in too soon and give an answer instead of letting silence do the work.

3. They Fear Losing Control

☐ But true control comes from understanding and talking with purpose; you don't need control just for the sake of it.

How to Actually Listen Instead of Just Waiting to Speak

1. Pause Before Responding

☐ Give them space in which to elaborate - you'll be surprised what additional information they reveal.

2. Mirror Key Phrases

☐ *"You said your team is struggling with consistency - how do you mean?"*

3. Let Silence Do the Work

☐ Prospects often fill the gap with deeper insights if you don't rush in.

The Bottom Line

Average reps listen just enough to respond. Strong reps listen to understand. If you're planning your next question instead of absorbing their answer, you're not really listening.

Prescribing Too Soon - Solving the Wrong Problem

As we said, the best salespeople think like doctors. They diagnose first, and prescribe second. Average reps rush to a solution before they fully understand the problem. The solution they offer is also always the one that they're most comfortable selling. Strong reps take the time to diagnose properly, ensuring their recommendation actually fits, and that the prospect is truly qualified.

What Prescribing Too Soon Sounds Like

Example:

- **Prospect:** *"Our team struggles with prospecting."*
- **Average rep:** *"Got it! Our automated prospecting platform will help with that."*
- **Strong rep:** *"What part of prospecting are they struggling with specifically?"*

One assumes. The other investigates.

Why Reps Prescribe Too Soon

1. **They Think Speed = Value**
   - ☐ A fast answer doesn't mean it's the right answer.
2. **They Feel Pressure to Prove Their Expertise**
   - ☐ In reality, true expertise is shown through great questions.
3. **They Assume They Already Know the Answer**
   - ☐ And they do this instead of uncovering what's actually wrong.

4. **They stick to what they're most comfortable with**
    - ☐ Too often, when prescribing early, the rep is suggesting the product/feature they're most comfortable with. It's easy, but that doesn't mean it's the right thing to sell.

How to Diagnose Before You Prescribe

1. **Dig Into the Root Cause**
    - ☐ *"You said churn is a challenge - what's making it a challenge?"*
2. **Validate Before Offering a Solution**
    - ☐ *"If you fixed that level of churn, what's the win here in pounds and pence?"*
3. **Make Sure They're Ready for a Solution**
    - ☐ *"Is this something you'd like to improve or need to improve?"*

The Bottom Line

Average reps pitch too soon and solve the wrong problem. Strong reps diagnose first and make sure their solution (if any) is the right one. If you're prescribing before fully understanding, you're just guessing.

Staying with One Contact - A Risky Bet

If you're relying on a single champion to get the deal done, you're putting your pipeline at risk. Deals are rarely won by Influencing just one person. Average reps build a relationship with one contact and assume they'll push it through. Strong reps multi-thread, ensuring they have direct access to the key decision-makers and influencers.

What Staying with One Contact Sounds Like

Example:

- **Average Rep (to their boss):** *"I've got a great relationship with my champion, they've told me it shouldn't be a problem; they always get what they want."*
- **Strong Rep (to their prospect):** *"Aside from you, who else cares about solving this?" "Is there anyone else that would feel left out if a decision was made and they weren't included?" "Who else knows we're talking?" "Does the CFO/procurement not need to get involved above a certain spend?"*

Single threading isn't an effective strategy. If your one contact disappears or does a poor job selling this internally, it's game over.

Why Reps Rely on One Contact

1. **They're Too Comfortable**
   - ☐ They build rapport with one person and don't want to "rock the boat" by asking for access to others. They fear more people will equate to more objections and risk.
2. **They Fear Going Over Their Champion's Head**
   - ☐ They worry they'll offend their contact by reaching out to senior staff, but real

champions, who are serious buyers, will welcome the help and split the pressure of the decision with others.

3. **They Assume Their Contact Has Influence**
   - ☐ Not everyone who likes your solution can actually sign the agreement. If they aren't a key decision-maker, they're a champion.

4. **They Avoid Tough Conversations**
   - ☐ Asking questions like *"Who else cares about this"* or *"whose signature is on the order form?"* forces them to confront the reality that their deal isn't as far along as they thought.

Ways to Multi-Thread without Losing Your Champion

1. **Ask Early and Make It Normal**
   - ☐ *"Who else cares about solving this?"*
   - ☐ *"Who else would feel left out if they weren't included?"*
   - ☐ *"Who else knows we're speaking?"*

2. **Get Introductions Proactively**
   - ☐ Ask them who else is likely to get involved and suggest you both get ahead of the game and take it to them proactively. Work with your champion as if you're on the same team looking for the same outcome.
   - ☐ If they say nobody, challenge them - *"Does the CFO not need to approve this? "Do procurement not need to take a look"*

"Does your legal team not need to approve the agreement?" Reps fear exploring these other roles, as they see them as threats - in truth, they're threats whether you talk to them or not, so embrace it and work with your champion in good time. Be proactive, not reactive.

3. **Make It About Decision Alignment**

☐ *"It's very rare for one person to make a sole decision on something like this; who else will get involved and how do we make sure we're all aligned on [problem]?"*

The Bottom Line

Your deal is already multi-threaded - people don't buy or make decisions alone. The only question is whether you have visibility into those conversations. If you're not proactively threading into multiple stakeholders, those discussions are still happening - just without you.

Average reps stay in their comfort zone, relying on a single champion and hoping for the best. Strong reps make sure they're part of the broader buying conversation, securing access to decision-makers and influencers early in the process.

If you don't thread it, you're flying blind. And if you're flying blind, you're not really in control of your deal.

Average reps stay comfortable with one contact and assume the deal will happen. Strong reps multi-thread, ensuring they have access to the decision-makers and influencers who actually drive the purchase. If you're relying on a single champion, you're one personnel change away from losing the deal entirely.

Bringing It All Together

The difference between average and strong reps isn't just about what they do - it's about what they avoid.

The Deadly Sins of Discovery aren't just bad habits. They're deal killers. They waste time, weaken conversations, and leave reps chasing prospects instead of controlling the sale.

Strong reps don't fall into these traps. They don't make the discovery call about themselves. They don't rush to pitch, accept vague answers, or cling to a single contact. They don't mistake politeness for commitment, or let the prospect dictate the call. Instead, they ask better questions, challenge assumptions, and take control.

The reps who master discovery aren't the ones who just know what to do - they're the ones who also know what not to do and have the discipline to avoid these mistakes every single time.

If you want to close more deals, fix your discovery. And to fix your discovery, start by cutting out the bad habits that are holding you back.

Chapter Fifteen

The Discovery Question Library

While we don't recommend running through a rigid checklist in every discovery call, having a strong bank of insightful questions can be invaluable. Great discovery is about having a dynamic conversation - one that adapts to the prospect's needs, challenges, and priorities.

To help you navigate these conversations effectively, we've compiled a glossary of discovery questions that we've found particularly useful. These are grouped into key categories, allowing you to dip in and out as needed, to guide the discussion naturally. You may notice some questions appearing in multiple sections - that's intentional. The best discovery conversations aren't linear, and the same question can serve different purposes, depending on where the conversation flows.

Use this as a guide, not a script. If need be, rephrase the questions in your own words, the way you would normally speak to someone. The goal is to uncover real pain points, priorities, and decision-making processes that will drive the deal forward. Keep these questions up your sleeve, adapt them to the moment, and use them to facilitate meaningful discussions that move the needle.

Setting the Stage *(Aligning Expectations and Establishing Context)*

1. **What's the reason we're speaking today?**
   This establishes their agenda and immediate priorities.

2. **What happened that day that led to you booking a call with us?**
   This uncovers the specific trigger event that created urgency.

3. **You must get asked for your time multiple times a day - what convinced you to spend half an hour with me?**
   This helps gauge priority level and differentiates you from other vendors.

4. **What's going to make this a valuable call for you?**
   This ensures the conversation delivers value based on their expectations.

5. **How does this [reason they wanted to speak] link to your objectives?**
   This connects their interest to broader business goals, increasing the chance of alignment.

6. **Who set you those objectives?**
   This identifies the true driver behind this initiative and who has influence over the decision.

7. **Do they know we're talking today?**
   This determines if key stakeholders are involved or if you'll need to multi-thread.

8. **What made you pick this moment to explore solutions rather than six months ago?**
   This pinpoints why this is urgent at this point in time.

9. **If this call were a total success, what would you walk away with?**
   This defines their ideal outcome, helping you structure the call accordingly.

10. **Are you yet to decide if you want to buy [your product] and that's what we need to figure out today, OR have you decided that you want to buy [your product], and we just need to spend our time discussing what that looks like today?**
    This distinguishes between evaluation mode vs solution mode, shaping your approach.

11. **On a scale of 1-10, to get us to where we need to, how direct do you want me to be on the call with you today?**
    This establishes how much you can challenge their thinking without breaking rapport.

12. **Is there anything else you think I need to know/would be helpful for me to know?**
    This gives them an opportunity to share context that might be critical.

Understanding Their World *(Building Context and Establishing Business Impact)*

1. **Give me a sense of your main priorities and how this fits in?**
   This helps frame your solution within what actually matters to them.

2. **If your boss/team was on the call, what would they say their biggest frustration is?**
   This uncovers pain points indirectly, and brings in broader team challenges.

3. **How long has this been a problem?**
   This determines whether this is a new issue or a long-standing challenge.

4. **What's changed recently that's made you start looking at this?**
   This identifies the trigger event that shifted them from passive to active buyer.

5. **[If the problem is less than six months old] - "Maybe it's just a glitch, why not leave it for another six months?"**
   This tests their commitment to solving the issue.

6. **Many people would like to fix that problem. I'm curious, for you; is it a like or a need, because they're different things?**
   This differentiates between a priority problem and a nice-to-have.

7. **What have you tried in the past to solve this problem?**
   This establishes their previous efforts and whether they've failed.

8. **Did it work?**
   This reveals why their previous solutions weren't effective.

9. **What are you currently doing to tackle [problem]?**
   This uncovers their current workaround and potential inefficiencies.

10. **Who else have you spoken to about solving this?**
    This helps you understand competitors or internal discussions.

11. **How come you didn't start working with them?**
    This identifies their objections to competitors or internal blockers.

12. **If nothing changes in the next three to six months, what does that really mean for you and your team?**
    This forces them to think about the cost of inaction.

13. **Would it be fair to say this is annoying, but you could live with it?**
    This helps differentiate between frustration and a critical problem.

14. Let's imagine we leave it, and I see you in a year's time and nothing has changed - how would you feel?

This drives emotional urgency.

15. Are you trying to fix this, or are you just looking for ideas right now?

This establishes if they're serious or just browsing.

16. What's the one thing you wish you could spend more time on instead of dealing with this problem?

This quantifies the opportunity cost for them.

17. Have you ever tried ignoring this issue? What happened?

This reinforces the pain of inaction.

Digging into the Pain *(Uncovering Root Causes and Personal Impact)*

1. If you could fix one thing quickly, what would it be?

This prioritises their biggest pain point.

2. If you had a magic wand, what's the first thing you'd change?

This discourages overthinking and gets to their core frustration fast.

3. What's the real blocker stopping you from solving this?

This identifies the true bottleneck.

4. **What's the most frustrating part of [current process/problem]?**
   This reveals their emotional friction points.

5. **How does this problem affect you personally?**
   This connects to personal stakes, thus increasing urgency.

6. **What's the risk of doing nothing?**
   This forces them to justify the need for change now.

7. **What's the moment you realised, "This needs to change"?**
   This pinpoints the emotional breaking point.

8. **If it's a people issue (i.e., sales team underperforming) - why don't you just let those people go?**
   This challenges their commitment to solving the problem.

9. **What else have you tried? I'd have thought that would have worked?**
   This challenges their logic, making them rethink their current path.

10. **When you say it's not where it needs to be - do you mean it's a "want" or a "need"?**
    This separates curiosity from urgency.

11. **What's the cost of inaction - not just in money, but in time, morale, or lost opportunities?**
This quantifies the holistic impact beyond financials.

12. **Who on your team feels this pain the most?**
This highlights internal champions who may help push the deal forward.

Quantifying the Impact *(Attaching Measurable Data to Their Pain)*

1. **What key metrics are most impacted by this problem?**
This links their pain to the business-critical numbers that leadership care about.

2. **What's the reason that matters?**
This ensures they articulate why fixing this is essential, and not just desirable.

3. **Just to get a sense of the size of the problem, can you give me a rough idea of the size of the gap here?**
This encourages them to quantify the problem, making it more tangible.

4. **Do the sums with me - what's the cost of this problem?**
This prompts them to acknowledge the financial impact, increasing urgency.

5. **If you could put a number on the impact of the problem what would it be?**
   This pushes them to assign a value, reinforcing the need for action.

6. **Help me understand the cost of this problem in pounds and pence.**
   This turns an abstract issue into a clear financial problem.

7. **[Whatever figure they say] "Is that a lot of money to the business?"**
   This forces them to internalise the severity of the cost.

8. **What happens if you get that /avoid that?**
   This gets them to imagine the consequences of action or inaction.

9. **If we fast-forward a year and this is still a problem, what does that mean for you?**
   This creates a long-term pain narrative, making inaction less attractive.

10. **How much time are you or your team spending on workarounds?**
    This identifies hidden costs in wasted hours and inefficiencies.

11. **How does this compare to what your competitors are doing? Are they ahead or facing similar issues?**
    This introduces competitive FOMO, increasing urgency.

12. **That feels like a big issue. If it's been that way for months/years is it fair to say this isn't such a big problem?**

    This checks whether they truly see this as critical or just tolerable.

13. **If you could free up X hours per week/ month, what difference would that make?**

    This shifts their focus to the opportunity cost of inaction.

14. **How does this problem impact team morale?**

    This connects the issue to employee frustration and retention.

15. **How would solving this problem change the way your team operates day-to-day?**

    This makes them visualise the real-world improvements of a solution.

16. **If this problem didn't exist, what would your team be able to achieve instead?**

    This frames the conversation around growth and possibilities, rather than just fixing a problem.

17. **How does this issue make you look to your leadership/customers/peers?**

    This taps into personal and professional stakes, like their reputation, credibility, and stress

Decision-Making and Buying Process *(Mapping the Path to a Signed Deal)*

1. **Talk me through how decisions like this typically get made in your world.**
   This establishes their internal buying process and where deals can stall.

2. **Who else needs to be involved to make this happen?**
   This identifies key decision-makers early to avoid surprises later.

3. **I've come to learn that if X person is left out, it runs the risk of a poor rollout. Should we make sure they are included in our next call?**
   This helps with multi-threading, while framing it as avoiding failure, rather than selling.

4. **Who else cares about solving this?**
   This expands the stakeholder map to uncover hidden influencers.

5. **Who would feel disappointed if they were left out of our next meeting?**
   This subtly encourages them to involve key players without forcing it.

6. **Who in the business has had conversations around solving this?**
   This shows whether other teams have already discussed solutions internally.

7. **Do they know we're speaking today?**
   This determines if you're operating in a silo, or if leadership is already involved.

8. **Who and what can stop this from happening? What's the reason they'd stop it?**
   This identifies deal blockers early so they can be proactively addressed.

9. **If you decide this is the right way forward, what needs to happen internally first?**
   This gets clarity on next steps, so you don't rely on assumptions.

10. **How do you usually buy things like this?**
    This confirms if they have a structured procurement process.

11. **If we were having this same conversation in six months and nothing had moved forward, what would be the reason?**
    This surfaces potential roadblocks that could stall the deal.

12. **Have you rolled out something similar be fore? What worked, and what didn't?**
    This uncovers previous experiences that may influence their decision-making.

13. **Who ultimately signs this off? [Followed by] so it would be their signature on the order form?**
    This pinpoints who holds final approval power.

14. **If they [the DM] say no, is this dead?**
    This tests their commitment and alternative options if it gets rejected.

15. **And if they say yes, would we be working together?**
    This pushes for verbal commitment.

16. **And just so I understand, what would be the reasons you'd say we'd be working together?**
    This gets them to put the reasons why they want to move forward in their own words, reinforcing their intent.

17. **When you go to your CFO, what's the argument you're making for this investment?**
    This helps pre-empt financial objections before they arise.

18. **Just so I understand - what's the best- and worst-case scenario for you here?**
    Frames their decision in terms of risk vs reward.

Handling Objections and Concerns (*Addressing Roadblocks Before They Kill the Deal*)

1. **What's your biggest hesitation about moving forward with this?**
   This reveals underlying concerns before they become deal-breakers.

2. **If we could solve [specific concern], would that remove any hesitation?**
   This tests whether the concern is real or just a delaying tactic.

3. **What other options are you looking at?**
   This identifies competition and where you stand in the evaluation process.

4. **What's stopping this from being a top priority right now?**
   This reveals competing priorities that could stall the deal.

5. **If budget weren't an issue, would this be an obvious yes?**
   This determines whether cost is the real objection or just an excuse.

6. **Have you seen something like this fail before? What happened?**
   This helps you address scepticism and de-risk the decision.

7. **How would you explain this investment to your CFO?**
   This ensures they can sell and justify the expenditure internally.

8. **If someone internally pushes back on this, what do you think their main concern would be?**
   This identifies hidden internal objections.

9. **What's the worst-case scenario you're trying to avoid?**

   This allows you to mitigate fears proactively.

10. **Have you ever regretted moving forward with something like this in the past? Why?**

    This reveals previous bad experiences that might make them hesitant.

11. **Is there anything we haven't addressed that could be a deal breaker?**

    This uncovers last-minute concerns before closing.

12. **What's the one thing you need to hear or see to feel confident moving forward?**

    This gets them to articulate their final requirement for commitment.

Closing the Deal and Next Steps *(Securing Commitment and Creating Urgency)*

1. **If we get this in place, what difference will it make to you personally?**

   This helps connect the decision to their personal success, increasing buy-in.

2. **Who else needs to be in the loop before we move forward?**

   This identifies any missing stakeholders to avoid delays later.

3. **What would make you want to tackle this now rather than in a few months' time?**
This creates urgency by getting them to justify why this should be solved now.

4. **I'm sure there are some other hurdles for us to jump over to get this signed off. What can you envisage we need to tackle?**
This reveals any final roadblocks before they become deal-stallers.

5. **I don't want to get happy ears here. Are you saying that if we were to agree on this, then we'd be moving forward?**
This pushes for verbal commitment, ensuring they aren't just being polite.

6. **Shall we review the mutual decision plan together, to ensure we haven't missed anything off?**
This positions next steps as a collaborative process, making it feel like a shared effort rather than a sales close.

7. **Once this is signed off, what's the last possible day you'd want this in place by? Why not later?**
This establishes a go-live date, reinforcing urgency and securing a clear timeline.

Future Vision *(Reinforcing the Value of Change and Ensuring Long-Term Success)*

1. **If we work together, what does success look like in six months?**

   This encourages them to visualise the positive impact, solidifying the decision.

2. **What would make you look back in a year and say, "That was one of the best decisions we made"?**

   This strengthens their emotional commitment to moving forward.

3. **If this works exactly as you hope, what will be different for you and the team?**

   This reinforces the tangible benefits of solving the problem.

4. **What's the one thing that could derail this, and how do we get ahead of it?**

   This pre-empts potential risks before they cause issues, showing proactive thinking.

5. **When should we check in to make sure you're seeing the impact you expect?**

   This ensures post-sale accountability, keeping them engaged beyond the purchase.

6. **If you made progress here, where do you think we could focus next?**

   This opens up the conversation for future expansion opportunities.

7. **If you had this taken care of, what else will that free you up to focus on?**
   This highlights the broader strategic impact of your solution beyond just solving their immediate pain.

Additional Questions *(Handling Objections and Deepening Engagement)*

1. **Can I ask a direct question?**
   This gains permission to challenge their thinking, making tough questions more acceptable.

2. **Can I give you my opinion here?**
   This positions you as a trusted advisor, rather than just another salesperson.

3. **Are you open to me challenging your thinking on that?**
   This allows for constructive tension, helping them re-evaluate assumptions.

4. **Would you like a different perspective on this?**
   This creates an opportunity to introduce alternative solutions that they might not have considered.

5. **Would it help if I shared an example of how someone else approached this?**
   This uses social proof to reassure them and build confidence in your approach.

6. **Can I push back on that for a moment?**
   This opens the door to handling objections gracefully without seeming confrontational.

7. **I've seen this play out before - mind if I share what happened?**
   This makes your insight feel less like a sales pitch and more like experience-based advice.

8. **Just to clarify - are we on the same page with X?**
   This ensures there's no misunderstanding before progressing further.

9. **Can I be blunt with you?**
   This prepares them for a direct challenge, while gaining permission to speak openly.

Discovery is about getting to the truth - what really matters, why it matters, and what is stopping them from solving it. Use these questions to steer the conversation, uncover real priorities, and move the deal forward with clarity.

The Final Word

If you've made it this far - thank you. We hope *'Deconstructing Discovery'* has been a valuable guide, full of practical insights and a few lightbulb moments along the way. Whether you're new to sales or a seasoned pro, discovery is a skill that rewards those who are willing to go deeper into the customer's world, into their challenges, and into their goals.

As you close this book, remember: while the world of sales may seem to be getting more complex with new competitors, longer cycles, and more decision-makers - the foundation remains incredibly human. Great discovery isn't about having the perfect question list or a polished pitch. It's about presence. It's about *listening* with intent, *asking* with curiosity, and showing *empathy* without agenda.

In today's world of rapid-fire emails and templated outreach, those three traits - listening, curiosity, and empathy, are more powerful than ever. They cut through noise. They build trust. And they lead to better conversations, which lead to better outcomes.

But this isn't something you just read about and suddenly master.

One of the most important takeaways we hope you leave with is this: you are never the finished article. Discovery is not a script to memorise, but a mindset to continually sharpen. Every conversation you have is a chance to improve - to reflect, to adapt, and to learn something new about your buyer, your profession, and yourself.

And here's the truth most top performers already know: you can't do it alone.

Even the most naturally talented reps plateau without feedback. Without accountability. Without someone to challenge their blind spots. If you're serious about fulfilling your potential, you need a coach. Not just a manager doing pipeline reviews, but someone who can push you, support you, and help you develop the skills you can't yet see you're missing.

A good coach helps you connect the dots faster. They help you turn theory into habit. They help you turn good into great.

So, as you move forward, ask yourself: *What's the next level for me?* And more importantly: *Who's going to help me get there?*

Whether you revisit the principles in this book regularly or seek out coaching to put them into practice, just remember - discovery is never "done." It's a muscle. And when trained properly, it becomes your most valuable tool in sales.

Here's to better conversations, deeper connections with buyers, and more deals won the right way.

Keep learning. Stay curious. And above all remember: discovery never stops.

Who is MySalesCoach?

If *Deconstructing Discovery* struck a chord with you, you're exactly the kind of sales professional we built MySalesCoach for.

MySalesCoach is a marketplace that connects salespeople and sales teams with a curated network of world-class sales coaches - experts who don't just know sales theory, but have lived it at every level, from SDR to CRO.

Just like the book, our coaching is built around the belief that the fundamentals matter - especially in discovery. Things like active listening, curiosity, and empathy don't go out of style. But they *do* need to be practiced, refined, and reinforced. That's where we come in.

At MySalesCoach, you'll find:

- 1:1 Coaching tailored to your role, goals, and real-world challenges.
- Tactical Group Coaching where you can learn with peers, led by experts.
- Structured Learning Paths that help you build critical skills like discovery, prospecting, and leadership.
- Custom Programs designed for sales teams who want to level up together.
- And a community that truly believes in the power of coaching.

Whether you're an individual contributor looking to sharpen your sales skills, or a sales leader building a high-performance culture, we're here to help you develop the habits, mindset, and strategy to win.

If the book got you thinking differently about discovery, coaching will help you embed it.

Let's turn insight into action.

Special Offer for Readers of *Deconstructing Discovery*

To help you turn insight into action, we're offering you **3 months of free MySalesCoach Membership**.

- Access daily live coaching sessions
- Join expert-led group coaching
- Join our exclusive LinkedIn community for expert content

All you need to do?

Let us know you purchased the book when you get in touch.

Schedule a call at www.mysalescoach.com

A Small Ask

One of the most rewarding parts of us writing our first book *'Problem Prospecting?!'* has been hearing from readers who've taken the ideas from our pages and turned them into real results. The messages we've received about how the book has made a difference in conversations, confidence, and careers... they've meant the world to us.

If this book helped you in your selling efforts - whether that was landing a deal, asking better questions, or just feeling more in control of your sales process - we'd love to hear about it.

Here's how you can help us spread the word:

- Leave a review on Amazon - Your feedback not only helps others discover the book, it helps us make future editions even better.

- Connect with us on LinkedIn - We'd love to stay in touch and keep the conversation going.

- Send us a message - Seriously, drop us a note and let us know how *'Deconstructing Discovery'* has helped you. We read every single one.

Thanks for being part of this journey with us. Let's keep raising the bar - for ourselves, for our teams, and for the profession of sales.

About the Authors

Mark Ackers - Revenue Leader | Co-Founder | Author

With over 15 years in sales, including a decade in leadership, I've learned what works, what doesn't, and why most sales teams struggle, especially when it comes to prospecting and discovery.

When Kevin asked me to co-found , **MySalesCoach,** I said yes instantly. I've experienced first-hand how great sales coaching can transform a career, impact success, and change a family's lifestyle. That's why MySalesCoach resonated with me. It's why I wrote *Problem Prospecting?!* with Richard, it is why we've written *Deconstructing Discovery*, and it is why I share my insights on LinkedIn.

Sales is tough. Sellers don't get the help they need. My mission is to change that.

I'm still in the trenches - carrying a quota, making cold calls, running discovery calls, and closing deals while scaling MySalesCoach.

Experience and Accomplishments:

- Co-Founder and Head of Sales at MySalesCoach.
- Co-Author of #1 bestseller, *Problem Prospecting?!*.
- Named in the Top 50 Sales Leaders and Top 100 SaaS Sales Influencers to Follow.
- Former coach at Sales Impact Academy, coaching thousands of AEs, SDRs, and managers while building the SDR and AE curriculum from scratch.
- First-ever coach for TrainYo, training hundreds of people breaking into tech sales as SDRs.
- Accredited high-impact sales coach, working with individual reps, leaders, and scaling sales teams at companies like Hubspot, Outreach, Deel, Flexport and more.
- Host of the MySalesCoach Podcast 'I Used To Be Crap At Sales'

Beyond all this, the most important thing to me is my family - my wife, Michelle, and our two amazing boys, William and Charlie. Outside of that, I'm a passionate Manchester United fan, keen home cook (who once came second on *Come Dine With Me* - I'm still bitter about it), and partial to a good glass of red wine.

Richard Smith - Revenue Leader | Author | Sales Fanatic

With over 15 years in sales, spanning roles from SDR to VP of Sales -I've had the unique experience of co-founding a sales tech company early in my career. This gave me an inside look at the power of sales conversations as the ultimate competitive differentiator, and the ways that coaching can unlock untapped potential in sales-people. At MySalesCoach, I get to fulfill my true passion - helping sales professionals and teams gain access to game- changing coaching that can transform careers and businesses alike.

This role also sees me remain firmly in the trenches, where I continue to learn and make mistakes every day.

Experience and Accomplishments:

- Head of Growth at MySalesCoach - shaping the future of sales coaching at scale.
- Co-Founder and Head of Sales at Refract - building a pioneering Sales Conversation Intelligence SaaS company from the ground up.
- VP Sales at Allego - leading go-to-market strategy for a leading Sales Enablement SaaS company.
- Co-Author of #1 bestseller, *Problem Prospecting?!*
- Sales Impact Academy Course Creator and Coach

- launched the flagship *Cold Calling Bootcamp*, coaching thousands of SDRs, AEs, and sales leaders.
- Accredited Sales Coach - working with teams at flagship brands like Zoom, Google, Trustpilot, HubSpot, and more.
- Mentor for Startups - I have worked with regional startup accelerators to help "non-sales" tech founders with sales strategy, coaching, and direction

Outside of work, I'm a devoted husband to Ashley and proud dad to Riley. You'll find me on weekends at St James' Park supporting Newcastle United, or on the sofa, exploring the weird and wonderful world of craft hazy IPAs.

Printed in Dunstable, United Kingdom

63763378R00211